PRAISE FOR *REACH OUT*

"*Reach Out* helped nudge me to connect to peers and leaders I admire, something I'd been thinking about for a long time. The next three weeks of my calendar are already full of coffee and lunch meetups. I can already see opportunities for new roles, strategic partnerships, and expanding my network of like-minded professionals to learn from."

—DEVASHISH KANDPAL, VP OF PRODUCT AT SKILLSHARE

"Reaching Out was a wake-up call for me to reinvigorate my outreach in an authentic and modern way. I loved how Beck outlined a daily approach that is easy to follow and immediately impactful. As a 20+-year marketing executive, I realized I could be continually learning and gaining insight from others just by making an effort each day."

—MARY ELLEN DUGAN, CMO OF WP ENGINE

"If an entrepreneur wants to grow her business, she must expand her network. *Reach Out* is your guide to connecting with the right people, in the right way, and positioning your business for the success you have always imagined."

—MIKE MICHALOWICZ, AUTHOR OF *PROFIT FIRST*

"Full of wit and honest anecdotes, *Reach Out* is my almost-30-something woman's practical guide to becoming a 'scrappy, hustling, doer.' If you are looking for an effective strategy for building your personal or professional network, you'll find it here."

—LIZA LUCKY, RECRUITMENT DIRECTOR
AT TEACH FOR AMERICA

"I often tell people to stop networking like a machine and start 'relationshipping' like a person. What Molly Beck has crafted in her important book *Reach Out* gives everyone the strategies and framework to 'relationship' like a pro and the incredible benefits that follow if done right. I've seen Molly live and breathe the concepts of this book for years and the incredible success it has brought her. Let Molly teach you how to Reach Out and watch your career go to a level you've never even dreamed of."

—PAUL ANGONE, AUTHOR OF *101 SECRETS FOR YOUR TWENTIES* AND CREATOR OF ALLGROANUP.COM

"The concept of 'Reaching Out' has been proved to transform careers, yet for many it still feels daunting. Molly Beck is about to change that with this accessible, practical guide to networking. With *Reach Out*, she gives readers every tool they need to build and nurture relationships—and ultimately unlock amazing opportunities for their careers."

—ADRIAN GRANZELLA LARSSEN, FOUNDING EDITOR
AND EDITOR-AT-LARGE, THE MUSE

"From shy, organized people to outgoing professionals with chaotic schedules and less predictable calendars, *Reach Out* will be a helpful tool to all looking to build networks that help leverage and create meaning and mutually beneficial relationships."

—JENNIFER BEUGELMANS, VICE PRESIDENT,
FP&A AND INVESTOR RELATIONS AT ETSY

"Molly Beck has cracked the code on connecting, networking, and expanding our horizons. We all know that even one great connection can change your life, yet making that contact can feel daunting. In *Reach Out*, Molly Beck shares her secret formula for how to make it happen. Read this book and leapfrog forward!"

—SAMANTHA ETTUS, NATIONAL BESTSELLING AUTHOR OF *THE PIE LIFE: A GUILT-FREE RECIPE FOR SUCCESS AND SATISFACTION*

REACH
OUT

REACH OUT

THE SIMPLE STRATEGY YOU NEED TO
EXPAND YOUR NETWORK AND
INCREASE YOUR INFLUENCE

MOLLY BECK

NEW YORK   CHICAGO   SAN FRANCISCO   ATHENS
LONDON   MADRID   MEXICO CITY   MILAN
NEW DELHI   SINGAPORE   SYDNEY   TORONTO

1 2 3 4 5 6 7 8 9   QFR   22 21 20 19 18 17

ISBN 978-1-259-86091-1
MHID   1-259-86091-4

e-ISBN 978-1-259-86092-8
e-MHID   1-259-86092-2

Design by Mauna Eichner and Lee Fukui

Library of Congress Cataloging-in-Publication Data

Names: Beck, Molly Ford, author.
Title: Reach out: the simple strategy you need to expand your network and increase your influence / Molly Ford Beck.
Description: 1 Edition. | New York : McGraw-Hill Education, 2017.
Identifiers: LCCN 2017023810| ISBN 9781259860911 (hardback) | ISBN 1259860914
Subjects. LCSII. Business communication. | BISAC: BUSINESS & ECONOMICS / Business Communication / General.
Classification: LCC HF5718 .B426 2017 | DDC 650.1/3—dc23 LC record available at https://lccn.loc.gov/2017023810

McGraw-Hill Education books are available at special quantity discounts to use as premiums and sales promotions or for use in corporate training programs. To contact a representative, please visit the Contact Us pages us at www.mhprofessional.com.

Here's to the babies in a brand new world
Here's to the beauty of the stars
Here's to the travellers on the open road
Here's to the dreamers in the bars.
—"Let the Day Begin," The Call

CONTENTS

PART III THE REACH OUT

PART IV TAKING IT TO THE NEXT LEVEL

AUTHOR'S NOTE

This is a story about wishing.
—RUMER GODDEN, *THE STORY OF HOLLY AND IVY*

This book is for the scrappy. The hustlers. The doers. Or the wannabe scrappy, hustling doers. This is for the people who just moved to a new city. It's also for the people who want to start a new friendship, want to embark on a new career, or just want a fresh start. *Reach Out* is for the people who are wishing for a better, bigger life.

To get all this and more, you are going to start Reaching Out.

Reaching Out means pushing your network to be larger by strengthening ties that already exist, even if those ties seem very loose right now. Reaching Out is not just spamming a famous person to write you back; instead, it's thinking strategically about the people you have already met, the people you could make a deeper connection with, and the people your current connections could introduce you to, to help further your goals.

There is deep power in digging into your network to push yourself toward your professional dreams, and most of that power is through acquaintances whom you know loosely, individuals whom you have met in passing, and friends of friends. These connections are *the edge of your network*.

The edge is where most of this power resides. Sure, you can write someone famous, and that person might write you back—but you're more likely to get a positive, truly helpful response from your aunt's coworker or the professor you had five years ago. That's because this person is someone you are already loosely connected to right now, at this very moment.

Together we are going to create a Reach Out Strategy Plan that will take you where you want to be. This plan uses only digital tools and costs no money to start or execute. And you can begin as soon as you finish this book.

I'm going to help you. The people you will meet or reconnect with because you Reached Out will help you. But most of all, you will help yourself by not being afraid to go to the edge of your network—the place where the action is.

The more people you know, the more stuff you can get done. It's as simple as that.

This book's focus is narrow. It's not about how to strike up conversations with people at the grocery store, how to throw a networking happy hour, or how to rock an interview. It's simply about how to leverage two tools—time and an internet connection—to expand the number of people you know.

The life you are dreaming and wishing and hoping for is within reach. You just need to meet some people who will help you get there.

Reaching Out is simple, something you can master, and you can start the second you close this book.

Are you in?

Good.

Let's do this.

INTRODUCTION

Having a Reach Out Strategy Plan has dramatically changed my career—without parallel, for the better. And with a minimal amount of work, Reaching Out can change your life too.

HOW I GOT HERE

In March 2016, I shared my story on Forbes.com as part of Denise Restauri's "Mentoring Moments," a column where interviewees share a special moment when something clicked in their professional lives and how it changed their outlook moving forward.

My column focused on a night about two years after I'd moved to New York City out of college. I was at a party in the East Village, talking to a man who was having a lot of success in his field, which I think was maybe finance or consulting. He wasn't anyone I knew very well, and I never saw him again after that night.

But as we chatted, I was struck with the idea that the reason he was having success was not because he was particularly amazing at his job but because he knew the right people. At first, that really bothered me, because I'd assumed—maybe incorrectly, maybe not—that he was using the old boys' club and his parents' network. Meanwhile I (who am neither old nor male) live in a city and work in an industry in which neither of my parents can be particularly helpful in terms of connections. (In terms of support, my parents are incredible. But they are both engineers who live in Massachusetts, and I work in media in New York City.)

For the next week, I kept thinking about my conversation with him. If this person was successful because of whom he knew, why couldn't *I* be successful for the same reason? Sure, I would need to put in a little more work than he did to make it happen, but if the secret to success is knowing more people *and* having them know me, then I'd just have to know more people. And the more people I knew, the more I could ask for help, so maybe I could even land a new job or get a promotion at work, find a mentor, or just make more friends (I desperately needed the last two). The way of the world seemed to be driven by the people I knew: I could rail against it, or I could work with it.

It was time to put in some elbow grease and make this happen. Creating my own network from scratch rather than through my parents' or my nonexistent Ivy League connections would be incredibly freeing: I'd design my ideal community of people I want to know.

So I decided that every weekday I would Reach Out to someone new. I was already Reaching Out on a much smaller scale—*maybe* once a month—but I wanted to really level it up. I'd mainly use email and social media since they are free and I could do them discreetly at my desk at work each day. About a week after the party, I put "RO," short for "Reach Out," into my calendar as a recurring task Monday through Friday and gave it no end date.

It's been about six years since that party changed my entire mindset about how to get ahead. I've been Reaching Out daily for years now, and this strategy alone has single-handedly changed my professional career trajectory and, by extension, my life. Reaching Out to people on the edge of my network has brought me more opportunities than anything else I've ever done to further my career—and that includes submitting job applications, applying to speak at conferences, and attending networking parties. My life has become bigger, not smaller, because I Reach Out each and every day of the workweek.

———

So when Denise asked me to share a moment in my career when everything leveled up, I chose that party and the subsequent adding of RO to my calendar each day, which I hadn't really told anyone about up to that point.

I never could have imagined the reaction I got from that article. It went viral overnight. My inbox exploded with emails, LinkedIn messages, Facebook messages, and tweets from people hungry to know more about Reaching Out.

So this book expands on exactly that—Reaching Out. But I also hope it's so much more than that for you. I hope this is a rallying cry for taking control of your professional future by taking control of your network. There is no catch, no software you need to buy, no payments of $29.99 due at a later date. All you need is an investment in time and a willingness to push past sweaty palms and shaky hands when you send that first email to someone you don't too well, or at all . . . yet.

MY FRIENDS ARE JON, KATE,
AND THEIR EIGHT

A lot of the Reach Out Strategy I know now would have been helpful the weekend I moved from Boston to Manhattan in 2009. I moved straight from a cozy apartment with my Northeastern University sorority sisters to a sublet right off Times Square, where I didn't know any of the other four women who lived there. It was Memorial Day weekend, and my new roommates were all away for the holiday.

I spent most of the three-day weekend in the living room of my new digs watching a *Jon and Kate Plus 8* marathon that was being aired due to Jon and Kate's impending divorce. I am probably the only person who watched the whole marathon, starting with the very first episode when the babies were babies, all the way up to the grand reveal of the last episode where they announced their marriage was over. During commercial breaks it would dawn on me that I knew no one in the city, felt very alone, and was scared to Reach Out to any friends of friends to see if there was a cookout or something I could attend. Then the show would come back on, and I'd get sucked into the story line of six preschoolers going to the dentist and push the thought aside. By the end of the long weekend, Jon and Kate's marriage was over, and it looked like my social life was too.

> *We are all in the gutter, but some of us*
> *are looking at the stars.*
> —OSCAR WILDE, *LADY WINDERMERE'S FAN*

PUTTING DOWN THE TV REMOTE, STARTING A "CAREER"

Memorial Day weekend ended, and my "job" of working two days a week in an unpaid internship began. I moved to New York City for the opportunity I hoped living there would bring; I had some money saved from working during school the past few years, but that was it. My semigenius, semi-insane plan was to do this internship until I somehow pole-vaulted myself to a better job. (After I explained this plan to my parents, my mom gently reminded me that I was in an ankle brace the spring of my senior year of high school because of a pole-vaulting injury in my one and only attempt to do high school sports.)

The internship was just for the summer, so I was already freaking out about having to move back home at the end of August if I couldn't find a "real job." Despite having some previous, decent work experiences, I was hitting dead end after dead end in landing a full-time gig. After applying to so, so many jobs, I finally landed one at a start-up that did sales recruitment for other businesses. This is a very fancy way of saying I did *a lot* of cold calling. If you had sales experience, lived in Texas (my main territory), and were enjoying your day, I definitely called you to interrupt it. But the office was located in Times Square, and I could walk to it from my apartment, so I was thrilled. I worked there for a year, but my main accomplishment was making my first Manhattan friend, Melanie.

I then moved over to a book company, where I parlayed my experience running a blog and my knowledge of how to send mass emails using a rudimentary form of MailChimp into a digital marketing job at Bookspan. I worked at Bookspan for about a year before taking a brief detour to Austin (just enough time to wear a crop top, live through the hottest summer ever, and mend a broken heart), after which I was back at the book company, rehired with a slightly better title, a small salary bump, and more responsibility.

Not too long after that, my former coworker, Clare, Reached Out to me, asking if I'd be interested in a job at Hearst Corporation. Shortly thereafter, I started the role doing social media and content for Hearst's Entertainment & Syndication division. Three years later, I moved to Venmo, a fintech company owned by PayPal, where I led brand marketing. I then left Venmo to start my own consulting shop. My recent clients have included Forbes, where I launched Forbes Podcasts, and Rice University, where I shored up its digital presence for some of its new media properties.

In retrospect, the point where my career really started to take off was when I had started Reaching Out regularly, right after being hired back at Bookspan (which was also around the same time as the party where I met that successful guy in the East Village who obviously had connections). Before that, my jobs had mostly been at companies you've never heard of and where the pay wasn't amazing. But being rehired at Bookspan was a direct result of staying in touch with old coworkers, which then led to the Hearst job (which was also a result of my staying in touch with my network). Once I had the Hearst name on my résumé, I was able to leverage that to the role at

Venmo. After having a few bigger brand names on my résumé, I could then start going out on my own and start landing clients as a consultant.

I still do a lot of consulting, but the big project I've been working on this year (besides this book you're holding) is starting MessyBun.com, a site that lets users record, edit, and find listeners for their podcasts, without requiring special equipment or skills (just like Reaching Out). In this book, I'll take you through parts of my journey launching Messy Bun by using Reach Out Strategy so you can see my own Reaching Out in action.

———

But let's take it back to a 2011 Reach Out that changed everything, and what happened next.

THE REACH OUT THAT CHANGED EVERYTHING

The Reach Out that first changed my professional life most dramatically is the one I sent below—and probably not for the reason you think. This was a blind email to an inbox of a (now-defunct) fashion site, Fashism. I wanted to start a conversation with the founder, Brooke Moreland, in hopes of writing a column for Fashism or being interviewed by her as a way to feature my blog, *Smart, Pretty & Awkward*, on the site.

Smart, Pretty & Awkward

Smart, Pretty & Awkward (smartprettyandawkward.com) is the blog I started while I was in college and still run today. Every blog post has three pieces of advice: how to be smarter, how to be prettier, and how to be (less) awkward. I link to articles that make me think, clothing I love, and books I'm recommending while sharing my own hints and tricks on how to make life smarter, prettier, and less awkward. Each post is headlined with a quote, which is a way for me to show off my love of sharing other people's words. (You can see that influence throughout this book: I have periodic quotes that inspire me throughout this text as well.)

Here's my email to the contact address that was listed on her site:

Hi Fashism,

I write Smart Pretty and Awkward (smartprettyandawkward.com), which is on track to get 240,000 page views this month. Would Fashism be interested in doing a blogger spotlight interview with me, or some other way to work together?

I'd link back to it on my website, driving my traffic of about 98% female, 95% US-based, and 82% between 19 and 25 years old to your site (numbers according to a summer 2010 readership survey of 845 daily readers).

Please reach out if you'd like to talk more.

Thanks,

Molly

To my surprise, I got a very nice note back from the founder, Brooke, who wrote[1]:

Hey Molly,

Sure, I'd love to talk more about working together. Your blog is great. I love the concept!

We maybe can do some sort of favorite things post? Or you can do a guest advice-giving session or something like that.

Where are you located?

She and I went back and forth for a bit and then decided to meet at Lillie's, a restaurant/bar in downtown Manhattan. We had a pleasant dinner, where we talked about the blogging industry and Fashism's success. While we were chatting, a woman at the next table overheard us and leaned over, saying, "Sorry to interrupt, but are you talking about blogs?"

This friendly person who leaned over was master connector Christina Vuleta. Christina is the founder of the advice site 40:20 Vision (4020vision.com) and is now the VP of Women@Forbes. After talking in person over our tables at Lillie's, I knew this was someone I wanted in my life. I sent Christina an email after our chance meeting across the crowded bar by contacting her through the address listed on her site:

> Hi Christina!
>
> We met briefly at Lillie's the other night; I write Smart Pretty and Awkward (smartprettyandawkward.com). The majority of my demographic (82%, according to a summer 2010 readership survey) is between 19 and 25, and I'm on track to hit 240,000 page views this month. If there is anything I can do to help you or you would like to work together, let me know! Your site is adorable.
>
> :)
>
> Molly

Christina's response:

> Molly,
>
> I love love love your blog! Would be great to get together and talk some more about synergies and shared advice :)
>
> Let me know if you'd like to get together for a coffee or cocktail . . . next week?
>
> Christina

We met the following week, and we just clicked. I call her my New York fairy godmother, and we have worked together on a variety of projects over the years, including collaborating on blogs and working together at Forbes. Beyond this, she's given me invaluable insight over the years on everything from when to leave Hearst to how to write tough emails to clients. She's so special to me, and I'm thankful every day that we connected.

Brooke, the founder of the site I initially Reached Out to, and I never ended up working together. But because I Reached Out to her and she was nice enough to have dinner with me, I met Christina, who has provided me with amazing mentorship ever since.

One of the most important Reach Outs of my career wasn't even to the person I intended to connect with . . . but Reaching Out got me there.

IS REACHING OUT JUST FOR CAREER REASONS? NO

I'm writing this chapter right now in "my" Starbucks on the Upper West Side, waiting for my friend Jocelyn to meet me so we can grab crepes. We met because she Reached Out to me for advice on a job offer after Christina, the mentor I met across the table at Lillie's, told her that we should know each other.

Here is Jocelyn's first email to me:

Hi Molly—I just met with Christina tonight, and she suggested I reach out to you about a job that I might take with a start-up. First of all, congrats on the new job at Hearst!

Are you around this weekend in NYC? Any chance you could meet up for coffee?

Jocelyn

It's a short email. She name-drops our mutual connection, Christina, congratulates me on my new job, and tells me specifically what she wants help with. We got together that weekend, and now look at us—friends eating crepes together on a Saturday years later.

BUT . . . I ALREADY HAVE
SOMEONE TO EAT CREPES WITH

I know what you're thinking: "But I actually I don't even like crepes, and honestly, it sounds a little pretentious you eat crepes on the reg. . . ."

I get it. You already have family, friends, and work acquaintances, and honestly some of the people you already know get on your nerves occasionally. (No shame. It happens to all of us.)

So *why* do you need to know even more people, some of whom will invariably get on your nerves eventually too?

Because increasing your network means increasing the chance for new opportunities to come in. If opportunities are islands, people in your network are the bridges that will help you get to the islands faster. Sure, you can try swimming, but wouldn't you rather take a nice walk over a beautiful bridge than be floundering in the water all alone?

THE KEY PART OF THE REACH OUT STRATEGY

If you think back, you have probably Reached Out to someone at some point. Maybe your college counselor encouraged you to Reach Out to someone at the graduate school you were considering attending, you emailed a blogger you like to ask for advice on something, or you sent a LinkedIn message to the hiring manager at a job you really wanted. So you've probably sent a Reach Out or two at some point.

But to make your Reach Out Strategy Plan successful, it can't be a one-off event . . . it's daily. It's on a schedule. It's so automated that you don't need to think about it. This helps with time management so you can respond to replies faster, and it helps because not every Reach Out will be a winner, so the more irons in the fire, the better. (More on time management in Chapter 10 and more on response rates to expect in Chapter 9.)

YOUR REACH OUT STRATEGY PLAN

By the end of this book, you will develop your own Reach Out Strategy Plan by following the prompts at the end of each chapter. (And the prompts are also combined for easy reference in Appendix B.) Your Reach Out Strategy Plan will include your career goals, the people you want to Reach Out to (these are your Targets), a list of what you'll offer and ask for in each message (your Gifts and your Favors), and personalized email and social media templates you can use immediately. You'll also find extras such as motivational quotes, a brief outline of your personal brand, and a schedule of how Reaching Out will fit into your life. We will go through each section of your Reach Out Strategy Plan one by one, so by the end of this book, you'll have it all.

SO WHERE CAN REACH OUT STRATEGY TAKE YOUR LIFE?

If you follow the plan that you will have completed by the end of this book and Reach Out to one new person each weekday, one year from today you will have made contact with about 260 people. Some of your Targets are on the edge of your network now, and a smaller number are complete strangers. Even at only a 40 percent response rate (and your response rate could be much higher), by the end of the year you'll have started new conversations with at least 104 people whom you have handpicked to be a valuable part of your network. That's incredible.

FINALLY, THERE ARE ALREADY TOO MANY BOOKS ABOUT HOW TO BE SUCCESSFUL, WRITTEN BY SUCCESSFUL PEOPLE

This book is not written by someone at the very pinnacle of where she wants to be. If you want to read about how someone became a titan of an industry via networking, there are plenty of memoirs and advice books for that. This book is different. *Reach Out* is for people who haven't achieved all their goals at any stage of their career . . . yet.

As your guide, I'm not where I want to be yet either—but I've gotten a lot closer since I started Reaching Out.

I'm in the trenches trying to succeed, and so are you—and that's the best place to begin.

///////////////////

TL; DR (TOO LONG; DIDN'T READ):
INTRODUCTION

- *The* key part of Reaching Out success is making it a daily practice.

- Following the prompts at the end of each chapter means that by the time you finish this book, you will have a completed, personalized Reach Out Strategy Plan that you can follow.

- If you follow your Reach Out Strategy Plan each weekday, one year from today you will have made or strengthened connections with about 260 people. Even at only a 40 percent response rate, you'll have started new conversations with at least 104 people whom you have handpicked to be a valuable part of your network.

YOUR REACH OUT STRATEGY PLAN

As you work through this book, keep two documents open on your laptop or two sections open in your notebook.

One document will be your Reach Out Strategy Plan, and the other will be your Reaching Out General Notes document. The specific prompts at the end of each chapter will go in your Reach Out Strategy Plan. But since

(Continues)

not everything we cover in this text will be directly related to your Reach Out Strategy Plan, have your General Notes document open to take notes on things you want to remember for future Reach Outs, on how to start a Reach Out Initiative, and more.

Your first task is easy: open up two documents or take out two blank pieces of paper, labeling one "My Reach Out Strategy Plan" and the other "Reaching Out General Notes."

That's it. We are off to the races!

PART *1*

BEFORE THE
REACH OUT

Chapter 1: WHAT YOU NEED TO KNOW
BEFORE YOUR FIRST REACH OUT

Chapter 2: JUMP-STARTING YOUR
DIGITAL PRESENCE

Chapter 3: FACING YOUR REACH OUT FEARS
AND DETERMINING YOUR TARGETS

WHAT YOU NEED TO KNOW BEFORE YOUR FIRST REACH OUT

"NETWORK" IS PEOPLE YOU KNOW, NOT EVENTS YOU HATE ATTENDING

Off the bat, let's reset what the words "network" and "networking" mean to you. Right now, both words probably conjure up something that seems unnecessarily stressful, such as a happy hour event where everyone brings stacks of business cards and most of us want to curl up in a ball as a direct result of all the small talk awkwardness. Push that thought away. Going forward, we will think of the word "network" as a shortened version of the phrase "the people you know." "Network" is a noun, not a verb. You are building your network by meeting other people, not meeting other people by networking. The former is friendly and attainable; the latter sounds like spam.

PREPARING FOR YOUR FIRST REACH OUT

Although you are probably excited to start Reaching Out right
now in order to get in contact with everyone, from your company's CEO to the person who knocked over your Valentine's
Day box in fourth grade and now works at Facebook, it's important to take a step back and make sure you are in the best
possible position to elicit responses from your Targets (the
people who will be receiving your Reach Outs).

In this chapter, we will go through key networking concepts. And in the next chapter, we will learn how to spruce up
our online appearance and present ourselves on the internet in
the best way possible—because you don't want to spend all that
time crafting the perfect online introduction to someone you
admire only to realize that you have the digital equivalent of
spinach stuck in your teeth.

Let's get started.

Just Become Beyoncé

Beyoncé is an influencer in the music space (um, and the
world, but for this example we will focus on the music space).
Beyoncé is a great artist, and she would be a great artist even if
none of us knew her name. But let's picture a world where she
was just as talented but didn't have the same network. In this al-
ternate and bizarre universe, the number of people who know
Beyoncé and her work is too small to recommend her for high-
profile projects. Because her network is too small, her influence
is small too. No performing at the Super Bowl or Grammys

for our girl! This (thankfully hypothetical) situation shows us something that is essential to understand—your network has the ability to make or break your entire career. The good news is that *you* are in charge of whom you know.

You want your influence to be strong enough so that you are the person others think of when they think, "Who is the most talented manager we have on the team?," "Who's an accountant who really knows tax law?," or "Who's that interior designer who could make this office space look awesome?" Striving to be the Beyoncé of your industry—both talented at your craft *and* well known—will help make you top of mind enough for decision makers and fans alike that you can achieve your own version of headlining the Super Bowl.

Somebody Else Holds the Keys to Your Dreams

One of my dreams is to be a guest on a big morning news program. I'm not there yet, but I believe I'm doing my part right now to make that happen while also being completely aware that if this ever does happen, it won't be something that is completely controlled by me. Instead, someone else who works at the morning news program will be the one to make this happen. So what can I do now to make sure I am prepared for whoever that person is? I am growing my network so that one day when this morning show producer says to friends over coffee, "Hey, know any guests we could have on the show that are doing something interesting?" there will be someone in that room who can say, "Molly Beck!"

Your goal doesn't have to be to sing like Beyoncé or to be a talk show guest, but whatever your goal is, it's still beneficial to think about the world in terms of relationships instead of robots. Just consider this fact: if a candidate is referred to a company by a current employee instead of sending in a blind application, that candidate is *hired* about two-thirds of the time.[1] Other people are the ones holding so many of the keys to making your career dreams come true.

Larger Networks and Other People Give You Advantages

To put it bluntly: *people and your positive influence over them are what get you what you want.* The opportunities you've been dreaming of will come to you . . . most likely through someone in your network.

This is a business book, so we focus mainly on how a larger network will help your career. But knowing more people doesn't only lead to new job opportunities, side hustles, or finding a mentor—it can lead to so much more. Growing your network can result in being invited out for someone's birthday, requests to join in on an Airbnb in the Hamptons, or a new dentist recommendation. Everything comes through your network, from business to social to personal. Everything!

The more people you know, the more stuff you can get done. It's as simple as that. Stealth is not helpful when it comes to growing your career. Unless your goal is to be a spy, anonymity will not help you achieve your goals.

Changes Come from New Attitudes and New People

Think of your network as a toolbox. The hammer is probably the most important tool, but it doesn't make sense to fill your toolbox with 12 hammers. You want to have tools for each type of job that might arise. It's the same when building your network. If you're a doctor, it absolutely makes sense to build a network in the medical community, but to be labeled an expert doctor, you must expose yourself to new techniques or studies, make an effort to meet with members of other practices or hospital administrations, and tap into other arenas such as publishing or politics that are looking for the perspective of a medical professional. Doing all of this will raise your profile—and label you as an expert doctor both in *and* out of your specific medical community.

Changes and new opportunities happen on the edge of your network (your weak ties), not with the people you are around each and every day (your strong ties). Working to broaden the edge of your network is more valuable than networking only with the people sitting around you at work each day.

Strong Ties Versus Weak Ties

Adam M. Grant, the author of popular business books including *Give and Take* and *Originals*, further explained the concept of weak ties and strong ties in detail in his essay "Finding the Hidden Value in Your Network" for LinkedIn.[2] I've excerpted a relevant part here:

Last time you really needed help, who did you ask? My bet is that you went to one of your strong ties—someone you know well and truly trust. Whether you're looking for a new job or some good advice, it makes sense to go to your closest friends, family members, and colleagues. After all, those are the people you can trust to understand what you need and have your best interests at heart.

But in favoring strong ties, you might be overlooking the strength of weak ties. In a classic study, sociologist Mark Granovetter showed[3] that people were 58% more likely to get a new job through weak ties than strong ties. How could acquaintances be more helpful than good friends?

The intuitive answer is that we have more weak than strong ties, so the odds are just higher. If you reach out to a few hundred people looking for job leads, chances are that most of them will be weak ties. Although this might be true, the evidence supports a more powerful explanation: despite their good intentions, strong ties tend to give us redundant knowledge. Our closest contacts tend to know the same people and information as we do. Weak ties travel in different circles and learn different things, so they can offer us more efficient access to novel information. Most of us miss out on this novel information,[4] filling our networks with people whose perspectives are too similar to our own.

(*Note:* Although in this book I mostly focus on strong versus weak ties, there is also a third kind of tie that can be very impactful, a dormant tie, that I touch on in Chapter 5.)

Your family, friends, and coworkers may be valuable people in your life, but they are not always the *most* valuable when it comes to acquiring new projects and bringing in the winds of change. That's where Reaching Out comes in.

THE ROLE YOUR INDUSTRY, CURRENT JOB, AND LOCATION PLAY IN REACHING OUT

There are some fields (media, marketing, and writing) and types of working arrangements (freelancers and entrepreneurs) that we frequently associate with Reaching Out. Working in those fields tends to be more fluid, as people tend to change jobs or need to hustle for more incoming projects compared with more traditionally stable fields such as law, education, or medicine. It might also seem like Reaching Out might just be for people who already have some experience under their belt or live in a major city. But no matter the industry, your current level of work experience, or location, Reaching Out can help move your goals forward. Here's why . . .

It's Not Just About Getting a New Job or New Clients

Reaching Out isn't just about changing companies or building your business—it can also be used to further your career by:

- Getting a promotion at your current company

- Being asked to speak at a conference or event

- Finding a mentor

- Being asked to *be* a mentor

- Making more friends at work

- Being considered for a new project at a current job

- Getting a new client—whether you work for someone else or yourself

These things are important, regardless of industry. Knowing more people—both inside and outside of your organization—will help you to achieve all of them.

I'm Still in School

Students who are reading this book have a distinct advantage over the rest of us: most people feel an affinity toward someone still in school and looking to get started in their field. Including your nonthreatening, noncompetitive student status in your Reach Outs can help you to get as much info as possible about a future career path and to meet as many people in the field you are interested in as possible. Reaching Out to Targets asking to shadow them for an afternoon or interview them for a "paper" (the paper can be real, or it can be . . . a paper for your diary) is a way to use your student status to your advantage.

I Live in a Tiny Town

One of the great things about Reaching Out is that you don't have to be in a big city to expand your network. Whether you live in a small town in Tennessee, a midsize city in Oregon, or Paris, all Reaching Out requires is a computer with internet and your time.

In fact, if there aren't a lot of people in your field in your area, Reaching Out to others who don't live in your city will probably be more valuable than connecting only with people who live near you (remember, these people who live in the same area are often stronger ties, so their knowledge will be redundant to yours, whereas someone in a different location may be able to introduce you to new people, projects, and opportunities). Instead of meeting for coffee or attending a networking event together, as you might with someone who lives in your city, have "in-person" meetings via phone call or Skype session—those can be just as valuable as a face-to-face meeting, and they are free (you don't even need to buy anyone a cup of coffee!).

> *You are the one who possesses the keys to your being.*
> *You carry the passport to your own happiness.*
> —DIANE VON FURSTENBERG, *THE WOMAN I WANTED TO BE*

////////////////////

TL; DR: WHAT YOU NEED TO KNOW BEFORE YOUR FIRST REACH OUT

- Think of the word "network" as a shortened version of the phrase "people you may know."

- The person that will say yes to your dream is most likely someone you don't know right now. Reaching Out can help you get on that person's radar screen.

- Reaching Out isn't just helpful when you want to change companies or build your business; it can also be used to help land a promotion at your current role, speak at a conference, find a mentor, make more work friends, and more.

- No matter where you are in your life stage or location, anonymity won't help you reach your goals. You can Reach Out even if you are still a student or live in a remote area.

YOUR REACH OUT STRATEGY PLAN

Choose your favorite motivational quote and put it at the top of your Reach Out Strategy Plan. Choose something that will help inspire you to push on when you may be feeling a bit stressed or overwhelmed as you first start Reaching Out. A few of my favorite quotes are scattered throughout this book for inspiration.

JUMP-STARTING YOUR DIGITAL PRESENCE

As I mentioned, right now as I'm writing this book, I'm also embarking on my other most ambitious entrepreneurial project to date: I'm launching a one-stop-shop website, MessyBun.com, that allows people to record, edit, and distribute podcasts they have created. I've never worked on such a large project without the security of an established company behind me before—and sometimes it feels like there is *so much* of a learning curve.

So for now, if you're feeling overwhelmed with a lack of digital know-how, I get it. The feelings I have when I'm trying to figure out how to choose what features to roll out with first or how to evaluate different partner options or how to spend advertising dollars mimic how I felt when I first started working in digital: too many terms, tons of different advice, and a feeling of general overwhelm. This is the digital know-how chapter I wish I had then. (For those of you who are already savvy when it comes to social media, this chapter can be a refresher for you—or feel free to skip ahead.)

GET A DIGITAL PRESENCE YOU ARE PROUD OF, FAST: EASY AS 1-2-3

So what do you do if you don't have much of a digital presence? Follow these three steps to get started:

- **Step One:** Set up an employer-friendly personal email address.

- **Step Two:** Set up or enhance your LinkedIn page.

- **Step Three:** Become active on (at least) one more social media site of your choosing.

Step One: Set Up an Employer-Friendly Personal Email Address

You need to have your own inbox that you can control forever. You probably already have an email address through your work or school, but when you change jobs or graduate, you most likely will lose your message history, which includes others' contact info. If you don't already have a personal email not tied to work or school, I recommend getting one with Google's free email provider, Gmail.

Your email address should be closely tied to your name and be as short as possible. The days of having your email address be pinkshoesunicornshirt@hotmail.com are long gone.

(Yes, that was my actual email address, based on my two favorite items in my closet at the time I created it.)

Step Two: Set Up or Enhance Your LinkedIn Page

Set Up Your LinkedIn Page

LinkedIn (linkedin.com) is a social media site that creates a digital representation of your professional network while allowing you to expand your network by connecting with new contacts. LinkedIn is a place where it's OK to connect with someone you've worked with in the past or hope to work with in the future, whom you might not friend on Facebook.

Almost anyone can use LinkedIn to their advantage when Reaching Out.

- **Job hunters:** Find people who work at a company where you want to work.

- **Side hustlers:** Make connections outside your day job to attract new clients.

- **Entrepreneurs:** Find VCs to pitch and look for partnerships.

- **Industry experts:** Connect with event organizers for speaking engagements.

- **Students:** Find people to shadow or have informational interviews with.

LinkedIn is the place to share your job history, professional achievements, and educational background. You can also write status updates or blog posts using the LinkedIn publishing platform to highlight your expertise, comment on others' updates to congratulate them on accomplishments, and join online industry or alumni groups.

LinkedIn is also a reputable site that Google and other search engines treat as such. Because of this, LinkedIn profiles usually appear (it depends how common your name is) near the top of online search results when someone searches for various combinations of your name, city, and/or current company. (*Note:* If you just created a LinkedIn page, your new profile should start appearing in search results a few weeks later.) The easy-to-find nature of your LinkedIn profile highlights the need for your profile to be up-to-date and able to show your credibility, so let's talk about three main things to keep in mind as you create or enhance your profile.

Key Items to Keep in Mind When Building or Updating Your Profile

One in three professionals in the world has LinkedIn.[1] So whether you are the one of the three and already have a LinkedIn page or are brand new to the site, there are a few things to keep in mind while building or updating your profile:

1. **Be truthful:** LinkedIn is a place to be honest about your job history. I mean, you should be honest everywhere, but extra honest on the World Wide Web because anyone can see your profile and easily fact-check you.

2. **But also be forward-looking:** It's also OK to highlight what you'd like to be known for or a space you would like

to move into. For example, if you work in sales but want to move into financial writing and have a handful of clips you can point to (even if they are on your personal blog), saying what your current job title is and also adding "freelance financial writer" works. Recruiters often search for candidates on LinkedIn, so having some key terms a recruiter might use to find candidates in the industry you want to move into is important.

3. **Ask for recommendations:** Having one to two recommendations under each of your past job titles is a way to validate your career experiences from the perspective of others. And don't stress about getting recommendations from your current coworkers; you don't need recommendations for your current job until you have left the company.

What you do today can improve all your tomorrows.
—Ralph Marston[2]

FAQs About LinkedIn

Q: Whom Should I Connect with to Start?

A: Now that you have a filled-out and enhanced LinkedIn profile, it's time to start making or increasing your connections. It's best to start with people you already know, such as:

- Coworkers from past jobs
- Current coworkers

- Vendors, suppliers, or third parties you work with in your current job

- People you have met who work in similar industries

- Anyone whose business card you have sitting on your desk

- Friends from high school, college, or other educational settings, such as certificate programs

When you add someone who won't necessarily recognize your name as a connection, I recommend that you customize the invitation to share why you want to connect on LinkedIn, or if it's been a while, include a reminder on how you know each other.

Q: *What Do I Say if Someone Wants to Connect with* Me *and I Don't Know Why?*

A: Here's what I advised my friend Jonathan to say when he wasn't sure how to respond after Sam, whom he had no clear tie to, requested to connect on LinkedIn:

> Hi Sam, thanks for requesting to join my network on LinkedIn. I'd love to learn more about you. Could you share some more details on what you're working on these days that I might be able to help with?
>
> Talk soon,
>
> Jonathan

It's as easy as that! This message starts a conversation while also allowing you to be selective about whom you are connected to.

Q: Is LinkedIn Just for Job Searchers? Will My Boss Be Mad That I'm on the Site?

A: I once had a boss who made an offhand remark to me, saying, "I better not see you on LinkedIn, because if you are, I'll know you're looking for a new job." As soon as he said that, I knew how out of touch he was with digital strategy.

LinkedIn is *absolutely not* just for job seekers; it is for people who are serious about moving ahead in their careers and care about building their networks to reach their goals (you!). If your boss or company has that "being on LinkedIn means you are looking for a new job" perspective, try to show your boss the benefit of LinkedIn as more than just a site for recruiters to find you. For example, send your boss an article about your industry you saw on LinkedIn and say, "Hey, I saw this on LinkedIn; thought you might enjoy." You can also suggest the site as a resource during meetings: "I'll look on LinkedIn to see if we can find that great new hire/consultant/web developer/other on the site."

Q: Do I Include All of My Job History? What About Where I Went to School?

A: If you're embarrassed about your work history (or lack thereof) or feel your current role doesn't showcase your potential, don't panic. There are work-arounds for all those worries.

- **Concern:** "I have a spotty job history."

- **Solution:** You don't need to specify whether a job is paid versus unpaid or full-time versus part-time. List volunteer positions, part-time roles, and clubs or parent organizations you were a part of (especially if you had an officer role).

- In addition to hard skills that would be valued in your industry, list other skills you've established (such as time management, mentoring, organization, or public speaking). You can also take the months off your jobs and only do years; instead of "November 2014–March 2015," put "2014–2015."

- **Concern:** "I didn't attend/major in/graduate from the same level of schooling as others in my field."

- **Solution:** There are a few things you can do here:

  - Take a certificate program at a local college or online and put that under education.

  - List your college major if you're less than 10 years out of school. If you're more than 10 years out of school, leave that off if it's not relevant to your current field.

  - List the classes that are most relevant to your current field and leave the graduation field empty.

  - Leave the academic history part blank if you have been in the workforce for 15+ years. Your work experience in the industry should be strong enough to speak for itself.

Step Three: Become Active on One More Social Media Site of Your Choosing

After completing Steps One and Two, you should now have a personal email address and a great LinkedIn profile that you are starting to use to build out your online connections. Finally, I'd like you to make at least one social media profile on another site. Popular social media sites besides LinkedIn are Twitter, Facebook, Pinterest, Instagram, Tumblr, and YouTube. Having a presence on social media is important because it provides credibility (you are who you say you are, across all platforms) and visibility (how others can find you).

If you're reading this book and you're already active on at least one additional social media site beyond LinkedIn, you're in great shape. If you're not active on those sites yet, this is great time to join.

A few tips:

- Try to also keep your usernames on these sites closely related to your real name and, to the best of your ability, have the same username across multiple sites. You can use Namechk.com to search available names across multiple platforms.

- You can also reserve usernames on other sites that you're not currently using just in case you may want to join in the future.

Use a password management system such as 1Password (1password.com) to save all your passwords in one spot and remind you of the social media sites you've already joined.

Which Social Media Platforms Should I Be Active on and How Often Should I Post?

If you're new to social media, start with two sites (LinkedIn and one more) and scale up if you are able to prioritize keeping the accounts active and up-to-date. In terms of which sites to join, here's a quick way to figure out which might be best for you:

- Do you love taking pictures? Join Instagram.

- Do you love sharing family and personal updates? Join Facebook.

- Do you love curating DIY, fashion, home, recipe, and lifestyle content? Join Pinterest.

- Do you have a specific hobby or interest? Ask friends with similar interests where they hang out online and join them there.

Try to engage on each platform you're active on a minimum of two times a month. To be sure you meet this minimum, you can write social media posts in advance and schedule them; a service such as Hootsuite (hootsuite.com), which is free up until certain limits, can help with this.

How Do I Join? A Three-Day Plan for Joining a New Social Media Site

When you first join a social media site, follow this three-day plan:

- **Day 1:** Register, fill out your profile completely, set privacy settings, and make sure your page includes a photo.

- **Day 2:** Go back with fresh eyes and revise everything after you've had a night to sleep on it. Try to keep your bios and photos consistent across sites, especially if you have a common name, so people can easily verify that it's you.

- **Day 3:** Think of everyone you know who might be on that social media site who would be appropriate to connect with. Go on a binge and friend them all. Don't wait and do it one at a time.

Whom Should I Connect With?

On the majority of social media sites, a key feature of the site is connecting with other users, becoming "friends," "followers," or "connections" of one another. A fear that I hear a lot about in joining a new site is "But I won't have any friends on the site right away." Usually follower numbers are public, and it can feel embarrassing if you have only two or three followers when you are seeing others with hundreds or maybe thousands of followers.

I once was talking to someone who works in public relations at a big agency about this, and she sighed and said, "The trouble with new accounts is that everybody starts at zero." So whether you're famous or just like the rest of us, everybody has to start at zero. Try your best not to worry too much about follower count in the beginning. I would try to have at least 50 connections on each social media site you are active on and then stop counting.

And though you should definitely connect with current coworkers, mentors, and professors on LinkedIn, it is generally not a good idea to do so on other social media sites until after you leave the company, *unless* you work in a more casual environment or have a real friendship outside work.

What Should I Share?

Here are some ideas for content you can share on social media to help solidify your online personal brand in a playful but professional way:

- Quotes—always a hit on both business and personal sites:
  - LinkedIn—business/success/productivity quotes
  - Pinterest/Instagram—inspirational ones
  - Twitter—funny quotes
- Behind-the-scenes and sneak peeks from new projects you're working on
- Celebrations such as first-day-of-work photos, birthdays or work anniversaries, or an office or location grand opening
- Community involvement or volunteer work you're doing
- Cool pictures of your office or office view
- A request for help solving a problem or for recommendations

Congrats! You have jump-started your digital presence by creating an employer-friendly email address and an enhanced LinkedIn page, plus you've become active on an additional social media platform.

DO I NEED MY OWN BLOG OR PORTFOLIO WEBSITE?

For both blogs and portfolio websites, you can create them easily with any number of sites, such as WordPress, Wix, and Squarespace. I would recommend paying a few dollars extra to get your own URL that is tied to your blog name or your name instead of using the default URLs that sites often give you that have the name of the platform in it (e.g., "yourname.com" instead of "yourname.wordpress.com"). Once your website is live, be sure to also include a link to it on all your social media profiles and at the top of your résumé.

But *how* do you choose whether to create a blog or a portfolio site? Let's look deeper into each to find the answer.

Blogs

I credit my blog, *Smart, Pretty & Awkward*, as being the launchpad for my career. The blog is the common thread that has run through my life for the past nine years. I've talked about it at every job interview I've ever had; having my own place on the internet helped me gain more experience faster in digital marketing, and the blog's popularity also granted me the visibility I needed to land opportunities to be featured in the press, teach blogging classes, and speak at events. Having said that, blogs aren't for everyone. The decision to start a blog needs to align with your unique skills and interests (such as enjoying writing) and your long-term goals (such as working in a field where an employer would value someone who came with an already established blog audience).

If you'd like to move forward with starting a blog, I have two main pieces of advice: have a specific topic area and follow the "three-month rule."

Having a defined topic allows readers to know what sort of posts to expect when they come to your site and also allows readers to easily explain to their friends what the blog is about (great word-of-mouth marketing). The other benefit of a defined topic is for you as the writer: knowing there is a loose framework for what your posts will be about can help prevent writer's block.

To make sure the blog is furthering your career, if you'd like to work in digital media or writing, focus on building an audience to help make the case to potential employers or literary agents that you are fluent in content creation to attract an online audience. If you'd like to work in another area outside of digital media or writing, have your blog be about your industry to show your credibility as an expert in that field.

Once you have chosen your topic area, follow the three-month rule: write on a consistent basis for three months without telling anyone. You can have the posts be live on the site and available if someone comes across it, but don't do any promotion until you know that you both enjoy writing a blog (not everyone does!) and have enough content that the blog still has momentum after 90 days. Once you hit day 91, you can start sharing with others.

Portfolio Websites

If you're less interested in working in digital media or writing, or don't have the time to write frequent blog posts, a portfolio website (sometimes also called a personal website) can show off your professional experience for potential employers or clients to find you. You can also have both a blog and a portfolio website: besides *Smart, Pretty & Awkward*, I also have a portfolio site that I use to get new clients for my consulting business.

Setting up a portfolio site allows you to show off your personality and work beyond a LinkedIn profile and can also help you appear higher in search results when a hiring manager or potential client Googles your name. Another advantage—the *Forbes* article "Why Every Job Seeker Should Have a Personal Website, and What It Should Include" reports that "56% of all hiring managers are more impressed by a candidate's personal website than any other personal branding tool—however, only 7% of job seekers actually have a personal website."[3]

A portfolio website can include items such as your bio, your photo, your résumé, links to projects you've done, a way for people to get in touch with you, and recommendations or testimonials from happy clients. (If you're asking people for recommendations on LinkedIn, you can also use the same recommendations on your personal site.)

What If You Don't Want to Create a Blog or a Portfolio Website?

If neither a blog nor a portfolio website feels right to you, Jenny Blake, the author of *PIVOT: The Only Move That Matters Is*

Your Next One, shares other ideas of ways to increase your visibility on the web without necessarily building your own blog or portfolio website:

> Public Original Thinking is my term for one of the best ways to become discoverable. What are you most interested in and how can you share that with others in your industry in a public way? You don't have to start a blog or a fancy website—maybe it's posting on LinkedIn or Medium once a month. Maybe it means writing a short e-book on your area of expertise, or volunteering to speak for free somewhere or host workshops, or be a guest on an interview series or podcast. If you're looking to get to know experts in your field, or have a topic area that directly relates to the type of clients you'd love to work with, you could consider a more in-depth project like writing an industry white paper. You will expand your network from the interview and fact-checking process alone, then will have a thoughtful finished product you can send to them as a follow-up. Now you're on their radar for potential future work, even if nothing materializes right away.

Still looking for another way to get your Public Original Thinking out there? Offer to do a guest post on another site. A big challenge with starting a new project such as a blog or a personal website is getting readers. Just like gaining social media followers, everybody always has to start at zero readers for a blog too. So if you find another website within your niche, offer to write an exclusive blog post tailored to that site's audience that highlights your area of experience and make sure you include your contact info in your bio so potential readers can access to get in touch with you or follow you on social media. By using this technique, you'll get the benefit of their audience seeing your work without having to start with zero readers.

Introducing *Peek into the Inbox of* . . .

Throughout the rest of this book, you'll see sections labeled "Peek into the Inbox of . . ." These are real Reach Outs sent by others who know the value of Reaching Out. Not every email or social media message featured will follow all the advice in this book perfectly or be 100% grammatically correct—and that's OK. "Peek into the Inbox of . . ." will show you how different people approach Reaching Out in their own words. The most important thing to learn from each story is that putting your own spin on Reaching Out will result in the best outcome, even if the sender doesn't follow best practices perfectly. Enjoy!

PEEK INTO THE INBOX OF:

Using Your Passion Project to Reach Out by Requesting Interviews

I Am: Natalia Levey, Tampa-based editor-in-chief of *Healthy Intent* magazine

The Target: Amy Porterfield, social media strategy consultant

The RO Type: Cool RO (we'll learn more about the different types of ROs in Chapter 5)

The Backstory: In 2015 I founded *Healthy Intent* magazine. It is my passion project, a way to connect deeper with the members of my community and provide them value beyond what I share in my newsletters and on social media. This particular issue was on building an online community, and I Reached Out to many industry experts for interviews or quotes. And to my biggest surprise, most people said yes. This includes Amy Porterfield, an expert on creating a massive following utilizing webinars, whom I followed on Facebook.

The Reach Out (Facebook Message):

> Hi Amy, first of all—I adore you and so happy you are finally doing videos! Way to crush your fears:)
>
> I've been following your work, and loving the Webinars That Convert course!!!
>
> I'm putting together the fall issue of my quarterly digital magazine Healthy Intent with the theme of community and interviewing online experts in their respective fields.
>
> I can't think of anyone who's done a better job at teaching people how to stay connected to their community using webinars or a podcast. I'd love to be able to feature some advice from you for my readers.

I appreciate how busy you are and hope your schedule would allow for this quick q&a.

The Response Time: 5 days

The Outcome: Amy's assistant wrote back that the interview could happen, so I sent Amy's team the interview questions. I tried to keep the process simple for them to be respectful of Amy's time. We set up the date for a Skype Interview, and the article was published in my digital magazine along with other incredible contributors. We also ended up connecting with each other as people during the interview, which was awesome!

///////////////////////

TL; DR: JUMP-STARTING YOUR DIGITAL PRESENCE

- Follow these three steps to jump-start your digital presence:

  - **Step One:** Set up a personal email address.

  - **Step Two:** Set up or enhance your LinkedIn page.

  - **Step Three:** Become active on (at least) one more social media site of your choosing.

- Three-Day Plan for Joining a New Site:

  - **Day 1:** Register, fill out your profile completely, set privacy settings, and make sure your page includes a photo.

⊙ **Day 2:** Go back with fresh eyes and revise everything after you've had a night to sleep on it.

⊙ **Day 3:** Think of everyone you know who might be on that social media site who would be appropriate to connect with. Go on a binge and friend them all—don't wait and do it one at a time.

YOUR REACH OUT STRATEGY PLAN

When people hear or read your name, what adjectives or phrases do you hope will run through their heads, either consciously or unconsciously? These are the foundation words of your online personal brand. Write at least three adjectives or phrases you'd like others to associate with you at the top of your Reach Out Strategy Plan.

When I did this exercise, the words I'd want associated with me were:

- Helpful

- Knowledgeable

- Generous

Other words I frequently hear from those developing their online personal brand are:

- Creative

- Leader

- Analytical

- Organized

- Experienced

- Expert about a specific topic

The three adjectives or phrases you chose for yourself are what you want your social media profiles, the content you share online, and the text of the Reach Outs you send to evoke in others. Your online personal brand succeeds when people use the same words you want them to use to describe *you* to describe your digital presence too.

If you're not yet active on social media, as you start creating your profiles and sharing content, run each of your posts through the lens of "Does this support one of the words that I want to be known for?" And if you're already active on social media, look at your last 12 postings across all the platforms you're currently active on with an objective eye. Taken as a whole, do they represent what you want your online personal brand to portray? If not, this is the time to make tweaks so your *next* 12 postings better reflect what you want to be known for.

The amazing thing about the digital age is that you are your own public relations person. So before you finalize your Instagram bio, hit "publish" on a blog post, or send a Reach Out message, think: Is this how I want to represent myself?

FACING YOUR REACH OUT FEARS AND DETERMINING YOUR TARGETS

T he first time you send a Reach Out, it can feel frightening. It can feel terrifying to send a message to someone and hope the Target doesn't take one look at it and think "What a *loser!*"

Here's the story of one of my own first Reach Outs to encourage you:

Right after I finished college and was hunting for a full-time job, I wanted to connect with and possibly work for Judy Kou Kasper, founder of Sunday Brunch Dress (SundayBrunch Dress.com), whom I had no prior relationship with. I emailed Judy after I moved to New York City shortly after I saw her work featured in *Lucky*. This was before I was Reaching Out on a consistent basis, and I credit Judy's kind reaction to this Reach Out as encouragement to continue sending Reach Outs, eventually leading up to my epiphany that in order to start seeing real results, I would need to make Reach Outs a daily practice instead of a sporadic one.

Subject line: Dresses Dresses Dresses!

Hi Judy,

Happy fourth! I found out about Sunday Brunch Dress through *Lucky*, and I am already hooked. I love the layout, the selection, and the "dresses dresses dresses" mentality.

I just graduated from school with a business degree, and I am looking for an internship or full-time work. I have pretty extensive experience in finance and sales (having done internships at both Goldman Sachs and Dolan Media's advertising department), but what I really want to do is work for a site like Sunday Brunch Dress. I'm sure, since you just opened in March, it's a small operation, but if you have any part-time, full-time, or internship opportunities, I would be so interested. I'm pretty good at social media as I run the social media outreach for a small company now, as well as run a fairly successful blog, www.smartprettyandawkward. com (I'll be featuring Sunday Brunch Dress on Tuesday, if you are interested!).

I would love to speak with you about any of the above—or just to chat about what it's like to run an online dress shop. Such a cool job.

Molly

I didn't hear back from Judy right away, so a few days later I sent the below Nudge Update email (more on this in Chapter 9), responding back to the email chain:

> Here is the link to the blog post I did today! Hopefully you will get some good traffic from it. Love to talk soon, Molly
>
> http://smartprettyandawkward.com/2009/07/07 /each-person-must-live-their-life-as-a-model-for-others-rosa -parks/

After I sent the second email, I got an amazingly positive response. Judy wrote back that she wasn't hiring, but she would be happy to meet me in person and hear more about what I was working on with blogging. We met the next week for coffee. We had a great conversation, and Judy was so sweet in person. Even though she didn't have a job opening for me at the time, we had a great conversation about fashion and career choices, and I continued to be a fan of Sunday Brunch Dress, occasionally buying pieces from the online boutique throughout the years.

As I was writing this book, I Reached Out to Judy and told her that her being willing to meet with me years ago is what built and grew my Reach Out confidence—so much so that over the years I'd continue to send emails to others I wanted to get to know, probably in large part because of the success I had meeting her. Judy was willing to answer some questions so that we could see what a Reach Out (RO) is like from the perspective of someone who received mine many years ago and who was so open and willing to meet in person:

Me: Was there anything about my email to you that caught your eye?

Judy: What I most appreciated from your email was that you had the majority of your education and training in business but wanted to apply your skills in a different industry. I took a 180 from the medical field and jumped right into an online fashion business. It's not easy to identify what it is you want to do and it's even more difficult when you don't realize what it is until later in life as I did. I was probably a little curious about your email too. I thought . . . .this girl has done an internship at Goldman Sachs and she wants an internship with me?

I also thought of some pretty helpful advice after you referred to yourself in a [subsequent] email that you were "super young and really have nothing going for you." I must remind you and your readers that everyone starts out that way. From your side of the table it may have seemed like I had things figured out. But, I was definitely still in the process of figuring things out! Heck, I still am. I have been involved with/helped with/witnessed several small retail businesses. No one knew everything from the get-go. It's a learning process. And more often than not, people are willing to help. Your email was honest and earnest. Hard to say no to that.

Me: Any tips for people who want to do their very first Reach Out and get such a positive response?

Judy: A little bit is luck. A little bit is managing expectations. If you email Anna Wintour, you may not get a response. Obviously you want to sell yourself, talk it up. But avoid going overboard right off the bat. Keep it short and sweet, conversational but still professional. I'd be much more likely to respond to an email that sounded like it was actually written to me and not copy/pasted. Do your research. Much more can be learned from a few well-written, sincere lines than an overdone resume where I have to bust out my dictionary. Grow a thick skin. Don't take it personally. You'll be pleasantly surprised by how friendly people can be.

I hope your first Reach Out is as well received as mine was with Judy. But if not, that's OK. Just keep Reaching Out for that response that will encourage you to keep going. *Remember:* If you're targeting the right people, they will be flattered by your sincere email.

———

For contrast, here's another email I sent around the same time that I sent Judy's:

Hi Courtney,

I found your listing on Freelance Success and I just wanted to write and tell you how much I loved your book. My roommates and I all read it and loved it—such a gem. Many of the ideas you mentioned I incorporate into my blog (with credit!).

So thank you for a great read! Please let me know when you come out with a next one—I'd love to promote it.

Molly

I never got a response, but I actually didn't even realize that until recently when I went through my inbox to try to find other emails I sent around the same time I sent Judy's. I've sent so many Reach Outs that I didn't have the time to get caught up on Courtney's lack of a response. Forget the Reach Outs that don't work out and move on: over time, only the winners stand out.

WHAT IF THE IDEA OF REACHING OUT MAKES ME FEEL SICK?

If you're outgoing by nature, you might relate to the ideas in this book right away and be ready to start implementing them without hesitation. But what if your personality is more reserved and you're feeling more nervous than excited about preparing for and actually executing your first Reach Out?

I totally understand that feeling. It can feel just so public and yet so personal to be sending Reach Out messages to people whom you don't know well—it might even seem like something you'll read about in this book and then never do. If it helps, I used to hate Reaching Out because of how nervous I would get before sending a new email or social media message. And to be honest, sometimes I still get that feeling. One of my hang-ups is that I sometimes feel a little embarrassed Reaching

Out because I don't want the other person to think that I can't do something on my own or that I am a burden.

But I try my best to push past these feelings and focus on two things: one, most people are flattered to be asked for advice or help, and two, stretching myself to push past those feelings will allow my life to get bigger and better in so many ways. I remind myself that the more people I know, the more opportunities will find their way into my life, and these opportunities are worth way more than the cost of being scared to send a message.

> *Do not be too timid and squeamish about your actions.*
> *All life is an experiment.*
> *The more experiments you make, the better.*
> —Ralph Waldo Emerson

THE "YOU'RE STUPID" EMAIL AND HOW TO PUSH PAST THAT FEAR

Recently, I was chatting with a high-powered Manhattan lawyer and telling him about this book's concept. As we talked, he said, "I should probably do that, but I probably won't." I pressed him and asked, "Why not?" I mean, he had gone to an Ivy League school and knew that Reaching Out could help his career. What was there to lose?

After a few drinks, he told me, laughing sheepishly, "What if I send an email and the person writes back something like '*You're stupid!*'" Then he added, "But it's true; that's what I would worry about."

I wanted more insight on this hesitation that so many of us feel about Reaching Out, even those of us who from the outside look successful. I talked to Megan Bruneau, a Vancouver psychotherapist, about why we might not Reach Out to others. I could relate to much of what Megan shared, and I'm sure you will too:

> The anxiety we feel around Reaching Out to someone we don't know is trying to protect us from pain. "Putting ourselves out there" in that way leaves us feeling vulnerable as we've opened ourselves up to feeling very uncomfortable feelings. If the interaction doesn't go as hoped, we risk feeling rejected, inadequate, embarrassed, ashamed, disappointed, or humiliated, and interpreting that rejection as a "truth" about ourselves. For example, "They rejected me because I'm not worthy of their attention/not smart enough/had a spelling error in my email." And if we're self-critical (which so many of us are), we have an even tougher time with those feelings because we beat ourselves up (e.g. "What were you thinking, Reaching Out to Dr. Famous? You're an idiot for even thinking he'd respond. You're a nobody—accept it").
>
> Cultural norms can also play into fear around Reaching Out. In some cultures, it's considered rude, disrespectful, and/or inappropriate to approach someone senior or highly regarded. If a person has grown up with the belief that they ought not to "bother" someone as busy or respected as X, or that it's disrespectful to assume they would have the time or desire to connect with

a subordinate, it's going to be far more challenging to Reach Out.

This makes perfect sense to me, but how can we push past these feelings? The short answer: make repetition the routine. Megan says:

> Exposure to uncomfortable feelings . . . over and over and over again is the key. The more we avoid uncomfortable feelings by not doing what causes them, the more power those uncomfortable feelings have over us. When we can become more comfortable with the discomfort (and remind ourselves they'll pass, however painful), we can open up to the risk that comes along with putting ourselves out there.

This is just another reason why Reaching Out daily is important—the more you Reach Out, the less power the fear of Reaching Out will have over you.

And if you're looking for a silly but effective way to boost your mood when you aren't feeling too great about your Reach Outs, try Googling "famous rejection letters." Seeing that everyone from Andy Warhol to J. K. Rowling has been rejected reminds me that I shouldn't take anything too seriously.

PEEK INTO THE INBOX OF:

Arianna Huffington

I Am: Sissi Johnson, Paris-based MBA professor, brand strategist, tech advisor, and editor

The Target: Arianna Huffington

The RO Type: Cool RO

The Backstory: In July 2015, a tweet by Arianna Huffington about women in technology caught my attention. I had just traveled from Paris to California, home of Silicon Valley. It felt like the stars were aligning. I did some online research and was lucky enough to find Arianna's contact information in an article she had written prior.

The Subject Line: Twitter follow-up + Introduction

The Reach Out Email:

> Dear Arianna,
>
> How are you? Yesterday, you tweeted about the importance for girls to learn how to code.
>
> I just arrived in California where I will be spending some time doing just that and meeting with Fashion tech startups.
>
> I would welcome the opportunity to share about Fashion technology and Fashion entrepreneurship on *HuffPost*. My credentials are attached for review.
>
> Thank you for your time.

The Response Time: 1 day

The Outcome: Arianna personally responded, saying she would love to feature me on *HuffPost* and cc'ing the Fashion editor to follow up. My first story was coverage of inclusive fashion at the Special Olympics and went live a month later, 2 days before my birthday. What a treat!

WHAT IF I DON'T KNOW WHOM TO REACH OUT TO?

The thought of sending a Reach Out email might be scary enough, but figuring out which people to Reach Out to can be just as daunting—yet it doesn't have to be. Setting your current professional goals is the first step in figuring out the people you should be Reaching Out to, and the Love/Don't Love Career List will set you on your path right away.

> *And please note this: You are never too old to set another goal or to dream a new dream.*
> —LES BROWN, *LIVE YOUR DREAMS*

The Love/Don't Love Career List

First, take a piece of paper and fold it down the middle. On the top of one side put "Love," and at the top of the other side put "Don't Love." Write down all the things that you love about your current professional situation in the first column, and in the other column write down all the things that are less than ideal. Then draw a line horizontally across the page under your Love/Don't Love columns; at the bottom of your Love list, brainstorm ways to incorporate more of the things you love in your life, and at the bottom of your Don't Love list, brainstorm ways to fix the things you don't love. Focus on ways that can be achieved (or you can make serious progress on) in about six months' time.

If you're having trouble thinking of items, these questions can be a starting place:

- Am I happy in my current job? What parts of it do I like? What parts of it do I not?

- When was my last promotion or salary bump? Is it time for a new one?

- How is my relationship with my boss? What about any clients?

- How is my relationship with my coworkers, including any direct reports?

- Is there another company or industry I'd rather work in?

- Whose job or role am I envious of? Why?

- Do I have both internal and external mentors?

- Do I have an internal sponsor?

Convert the List into Goals

Using your Love/Don't Love Career list as a starting point, formulate the things you want to change about your life and convert them into tangible goals. Good goals are SMART: *s*pe-cific, *m*easurable, *a*chievable, *r*elevant, and *t*ime-bound.[1] I find it more manageable to plan for about six months out when developing goals: it's a long enough time that goals can be achieved but short enough that I can still accurately predict what my life will look like then. Goals should also be something within your control and not dependent on outside sources.

Here are two examples of how this might look for you.

If You Wrote on Your List:

- Love—my company
- Don't Love—my exact job

  Good Goal: Begin Reaching Out to create or strengthen relationships with six coworkers within the next six months.

- Why is this a good goal? By increasing your network within your current company, you have a higher likelihood of seeing when there are open jobs or projects in other departments, *and* a stronger internal network can also help recommend you for these roles.

  Bad Goal: Wait around until your next annual review—many months from now—and hope that somebody hands you a promotion.

- Why is this a bad goal? If something is on your Don't Love list, you have a responsibility to try to fix it. Being passive is not a strategy for a successful career.

If You Wrote on Your List:

- Love—owning my own business
- Don't Love—stressing about finances

Good Goal: Reach Out to eight new potential clients a month to expand the company's sales pipeline.

- Why is this a good goal? By setting a goal focusing on expanding your network, rather than a pure sales goal, your pipeline and connections in your target market will increase, which will likely result in more prospects, referrals, and word-of-mouth marketing. All of these will directly affect sales positively without making sales your *only* focus (which can feel frustrating).

Bad Goal: Make more money.

- Why is this a bad goal? It's too vague and nonspecific.

——

As you can see, most bad goals are out of your control, too vague, or too large to complete in a time frame. All the good goals are *s*pecific (something tangible and not too big to be accomplished in the time frame), *m*easurable (you can always tell this because it has a number in it), *a*chievable (you have this in your control—not waiting for someone else to offer you a job), *r*elevant to your career goals (it has to matter), and *t*ime-bound (has a deadline). They are SMART goals!

Using Your Love/Don't Love List, Determine Your List Targets

Having your goals for the next six months articulated is the first step to brainstorming about the people to Reach Out to: your specific Targets, the persons who will be on the receiving end of your Reach Outs. Think: Who are Targets who could help you get more of what you love and less of what you don't?

Put another way, who are Targets who could help you reach your current goals? Think of all the different parts of the ecosystem you're trying to break into and list them all; as you work through the upcoming prompts, it will become clear to you which Targets are realistic to stay on your list and which are not.

////////////////////

TL; DR: FACING YOUR REACH OUT FEARS AND DETERMINING YOUR TARGETS

- Reaching Out *does* come more naturally to some than others, and that's perfectly OK. The first Reach Out is the scariest. After that, it gets easier.

- Reaching Out *is* a risk. But if you are afraid of trying anything that comes with a risk of failure, your life and career will not move forward.

- Over time, you will remember only the emails you send that got a response, not the ones that didn't.

- An easy way to figure out your current professional goals, which will then help identify the people you should be Reaching Out to, is the Love/Don't Love Career List. Take a piece of paper and fold it in half down the middle. On the top of one side put "Love," and at the top of the other side put "Don't Love." Write down all the things that you love about your career in the first column, and in the second column write down all the things that are less than ideal. Then draw a line horizontally across the page under your

Love and Don't Love columns, and in the bottom of each column brainstorm ways to incorporate more of the things you love in your life and ways to fix the things you don't love. Then, using the SMART framework, turn these notes into professional goals.

- Finally, use these goals to brainstorm all the different people who could help you reach your goals: your potential Targets.

YOUR REACH OUT STRATEGY PLAN

First, let's push past the fear that holds you back from Reaching Out: imagine the worst response that could happen as a result of sending an email to one of your Targets. Type it out and email it to yourself. When you do, you'll have gotten "the worse response" . . . and survived!

Now that that's out of the way, finish this sentence and put it in your Reach Out Plan: "My biggest fear when Reaching Out is _____. The way I will push past that fear is by _____."

Some examples:

- My biggest fear when Reaching Out is that the Target will think I am stupid. The way I will push past that fear is by having a friend double-check the first few emails I do for typos and clarity before I send them.

- My biggest fear when Reaching Out is that I will always be too scared to start. The way I will push past that fear is by setting a deadline to send my first Reach Out within 48 hours of finishing this book.

- My biggest fear when Reaching Out is that I don't know what to say to people. The way I will push past that fear is by following the email and social media templates in Chapters 7 and 8.

Next, let's focus on your goals and the Targets who will be receiving your Reach Outs. Pulling from your Love/Don't Love Career list, put into your plan two to four career goals you'd like to focus on in the next six months.

Under each goal ("Reach Out to five people who work in restaurant marketing"), list three to five different types of people (e.g., "fast-food mascots") who could help with each goal, and then get even more specific with two to four names of specific people who can be potential Targets ("Ronald McDonald, Colonel Sanders").

PART II

REACH OUT BASICS

CHAPTER *4*

THE GIFT
AND THE FAVOR

How many times around the holidays have you met with a friend, who—surprise!—brought you a gift? It never dawned on you that you were doing a gift exchange— you certainly never thought to bring a present. So you smile politely and open the gift, see the finely packaged scented soap (it's always scented soap), and thank the gift giver profusely.

How do you feel when you open the surprise gift knowing you have nothing to give back? You might feel some combination of flattery, anxiety, and embarrassment—but mostly, you're probably just thinking, "Man, do I wish I had a gift to give this person." And more likely than not, you probably follow up with a gift for the person in the next couple of weeks.

That emotion is the reason that you always begin your Reach Out with a gift. It is human nature to want to reciprocate gift giving. For many of us, we will always have that nagging feeling when we think about someone until we remember to reciprocate. And since the purpose of Reaching Out is to

55

elicit a response from someone we admire, the best way to get on that person's (metaphorical) holiday shopping list is to put the person on yours first by making a small gesture to help the Target's career.

THE GIFT

Why and What Do You Give to Someone?

Keith Ferrazzi, who wrote *Never Eat Alone* with Tahl Raz, said, "[I learned that] *real* networking was about finding ways to make *other* people more successful. It was about working hard to *give* more than you get."

The Gift is what you give the recipient on the other side of the email. There is a minimum of at least two things you should offer every Target you Reach Out to:

- **Gift #1:** A compliment, plus one additional gift from the list below:

- **Gift #2:** An article or book recommendation

- **Gift #3:** Knowledge you have access to that they don't or something special only you can create

- **Gift #4:** A press opportunity

- **Gift #5:** Free advice on a skill you have that would benefit them

Let's dive right into each gift . . .

Types of Gifts

Gift #1: A Compliment

All your Reach Out messages need to include a compliment to the Target. The compliment needs to mention what you appreciate about the person's work and also tie the work into your own personal story.

- **Boring:** "I liked your book."

- **Better:** "I liked your book because this specific chapter/paragraph/concept made me think."

- **Best:** "I liked your book because X, Y, and Z helped me [describe something you are doing or attempting to do]."

Another way to think about Gift #1 is figuring out what's special about a person's work and how it changed you. Then figure out how you can communicate that in as short a way as possible.

If you are having trouble thinking of something to compliment the Target on, put a Google alert (google.com/alerts) on their name or their company name. When an interesting update, product announcement, or piece about them or their company comes out, your Google alert will let you know, and you can be among the first to Reach Out and compliment them on the specific news and why it caught your eye.

Katelyn Gonyo, the owner of the online boutique Kiki's Bay, says, "One of the most generous things we can do with just our words is to tell someone how they've impacted us. It may feel like you're screaming into the void, but trust me: your words are reaching someone. And you've more than likely just made their day."

A genuine compliment is Gift #1, and all your Reach Outs should include this, as well as one more Gift from the list of Gifts #2 to #5 below.

Gift #2: An Article or Book Recommendation People Might Like

Sending people an article or book recommendation that you think they might enjoy subtly demonstrates to them that you share similar interests *and* that you are "in the know" with current industry trends or news.

The major caution with Gift #2 is to try not to send something that the Target probably has seen already. Link to articles that have just come out and share books that haven't been at the top of the bestseller list for weeks. Doing a quick scan of the Target's social media to make sure the person hasn't already shared the article or book can't hurt, either.

Here's a great email that was sent to my blog inbox while I was working on this chapter. It perfectly illustrates combining Gift #1 and Gift #2. The subject line was "Love your website!" and this email definitely got a response from me.

Hey Molly,

I stumbled upon your website from Twitter because the name is hilarious. I fell into a black hole as I checked out all your stuff (which as a fellow Millennial, is a compliment!) and I noticed we have almost the same taste in books. Have you read *Bitter Is the New Black* by Jen

Lancaster? It seems like something you might enjoy. Anyways, I just felt compelled to reach out.

Have a great Wednesday :)
Kirsten

This email has both Gift #1 and Gift #2 in it. It also has no Favor in it to start (read more about this below), *but* it opened up a dialogue between Kirsten and me that led to the opportunity for her to Reach Out to me again a few months later and ask to be a guest on my podcast.

> *Nothing will work unless you do.*
> —MAYA ANGELOU

Gift #3: Something That Only You Have Access to or Only You Can Create

This gift is dependent on the resources and information only you or you and a small group of people have access to. Some examples would be:

- A ticket to an upcoming industry event that you can bring a plus-one to. (*Note:* Anything you offer someone in a Reach Out needs to be for free. You cannot offer a ticket to an event and then ask the person you invited to pay you $40 after he or she accepts.)

- An advance copy of a book, behind-the-scenes look at a new product, or similar item that would be of interest to your Target and that you have access to but that isn't available to the public yet.

- An offer to introduce the Target to a person in his or her field whom the Target probably would like to know. For this to work, you must first ask the other person for permission to offer the introduction and clearly spell out the benefits to both parties.(See Chapter 11 for more details on how to use email to introduce two people who don't know each other.)

For Gift #3, you could also make something special that shows off your unique skills—something only you can create. Joey Held from Austin, Texas, is a content strategist, podcast host, writer, and, most important in this Reach Out, a musician. Joey issued a personal challenge to himself where he tried to see how many current NBA players he could fit into a song. With lines like "Don't hem and Hawes at me, I Acy all of my tests/And I'm directionally challenged, no matter east or West," the end result was 72 names in a three-minute song—not too shabby! He used the song as a reason to Reach Out on Twitter to Trey Kerby, one of the hosts of *The Starters* on NBA TV. His Reach Out included this exclusive song and got Trey's attention. The song was featured on *The Starters'* blog, and views on the song increased by about 600 percent in the weeks that followed.

Erik Kerr, the Salt Lake City cofounder of The Draw Shop, a whiteboard video company, also used Gift #3 to get someone's attention. When he was launching the Draw Shop, he and his partner, Summer Felix, decided to do a few free videos for influential thought leaders who had followings in line with their company's target audience. They sent one to Joe Polish of Genius Network, who loved it and shared it on his network, which generated free publicity for the new company. Joe then made personal introductions for The Draw Shop to places like the UN and Google. The company can attribute well over $2 million in revenue to the initial Reach Out email with Gift #3 that Erik sent to Joe.

Gift #4: A Press Opportunity

Being able to offer Targets exposure beyond their usual audience is an excellent Gift, with the note that this Gift is most valuable if you have an audience that's equal to or larger in size than that of your Targets *or* is in a specific niche they are looking to reach.

One way that you can (sometimes) judge the size of a Target's audience is by choosing the social media platform that you're most active on and comparing it to the platform that the Target is most active on. If the number of followers is roughly comparable (within 20 percent or so) to each other, it's safe to assume you have audiences that are roughly the same size and the Target might be open to a collaboration. For example, if a Target has an Instagram account with 10,000 followers and you're a frequent Twitter user who has 12,000 followers, you are probably *roughly* equivalent.

But . . . a secret? In all my years of interviewing people for corporate sites, personal blogs, and podcasts, only a handful of times has someone asked me the actual audience size before committing to be interviewed. In general, people are just flattered to be asked to be interviewed. It's always worth an ask, and if they decline, you can ask if they can recommend someone else you can feature. And as the next story demonstrates, even if the Target is a household name, if you are well prepared and can make a case for why your press piece will give the person additional exposure, he or she just might say yes.

Trista Harris, a Minnesota-based philanthropic futurist and coauthor of the book *How to Become a Nonprofit Rockstar*, went on a yearlong odyssey to find an opportunity to interview Sir Richard Branson. When Trista saw that he was speaking at a conference she was attending, she Reached Out to the conference events team with a proposal to interview him. The proposal included her background, the audience the interview would reach, the outlets the interview would be published in, the topics she wanted to cover, and previous high-level people she had interviewed. Because the benefits and her background were so clearly laid out in the proposal, the events team forwarded her proposal to the Virgin communications team, which then granted her request for an interview with someone she had admired for a long time.

Once the Target commits, whether it's someone as famous as Sir Richard Branson or not, make sure the interview is kept short and conducted in whatever way the other party wants (over email, by phone, by video call, or in person). It's also important to post the interview as quickly as possible so the momentum of the Reach Out doesn't wear out.

Gift #5: Free Advice on a Skill You Have That Would Benefit Them

This is a tricky Gift because not everyone has a skill set that lends itself to being able to give to others quickly or virtually. But if you do have a skill that you can help others with, make sure that you are up front about the skill being offered to the other person for free—no strings attached. A great way to phrase this Gift is: "Let me know how I (or my company) can be most helpful to you, and I will be happy to provide for free. My areas of knowledge that I'd love to share are X, Y, and Z."

Austin Iuliano, a Snapchat storyteller and content creator, shares how he gave Gift #5 and how that kicked off an important relationship for him:

> I was just getting into social media and building my business. I was active on Twitter, and one of my followers invited me to join a Skype Mastermind group. *[Note from Molly: A mastermind group is a curated community of people all in similar industries who brainstorm together.]* My reaction to being invited to the group was "Great! I don't know if I have enough success to really talk to people about online marketing yet, but I'll join anyways."
>
> One of the members of the group needed help figuring out his business' value proposition. It just so happened that this is something I knew how to do well, so I helped him out. My business partner's reaction to this was "Why are you offering free consulting? You could be charging for this." And my response was "Yeah, I probably could be . . ." But I honestly just wanted to help this guy out. The thought of getting something in return didn't really cross my mind, although if I was being strategic about Reaching Out, it probably would have. A few days after I finished helping him, he Reached Out and asked if I wanted to be his +1 at a TechCrunch event. My initial thought was "This could be weird." I would be

going with someone I don't know to a part of NYC I've never been, but I went anyways. And, that's how I met Alex, who is one of the coolest guys I've ever met, and someone I can now call a good friend.

A little while later, I saw that the site where Alex works was taking on contributors. I Reached Out to the editor, told her I was friends with Alex, and showed her a few writing samples. Because of the connection to Alex, she fast-tracked me to being a contributor for the site— and that kicked off my career in a number of ways.

Sometimes when you give first, something unexpected and wonderful will happen to you down the road, as it did for Austin. And even if that isn't the case, offering someone a Gift does allow you to hone your own skills *and* interact with someone you admire, which by itself is a win.

THE FAVOR

The Favor is what you are asking the Target. Although every Reach Out email must have at least two Gifts, not every email needs to have a Favor—sometimes you are simply offering a Gift(s) to be kind, or perhaps you want to get in contact with the Target because you anticipate needing a Favor down the road. The key to a great Favor is to ask a particular, definable question whose answer cannot be found on Google and can be answered easily in a paragraph or so via email.

What kinds of questions should you ask in your Favor? Well, some are definitely more helpful than others.

Bad Questions to Waste a Favor On

- Can I pick your brain?

    - The question is too vague, and for consultants who make money sharing their ideas, it's insulting to ask for their expertise for free.

- What open jobs does your company have?

    - Go to the jobs page and look for yourself.

    - Additionally, never attach your résumé without being asked for it. Always wait to be asked before sending anything as an attachment, because it can look too forward and also make your email go into the spam folder if it's your first point of contact with the Target.

- Can you mentor me?

    - Mentoring is a relationship that develops over time. You can ask for specific advice to start, but asking someone to be your mentor when you don't know the person well is too much to start with.

- How did you get where you are?

    - Who wants to tell his or her whole life story in an email, especially to a stranger? Plus I bet if you Googled it, you could find the answer or at least part of the answer in another interview or on the person's LinkedIn page.

Good Questions to Spend a Favor On

- What industry conferences or events do you think are worth the time and money to attend?

- What trends in our field do you think I should be paying attention to?

- What did you wish you did to get ahead when you were at my experience level?

- Were there any questions you didn't ask that you wish you had when interviewing for your current job?

- Are there any books that you wish you'd read earlier in your career that I should read now?

A Java Note

Offering to buy people coffee shouldn't be your initial Gift (it's not really a Gift; it's an obligation). If you've been emailing back and forth several times and are getting along, then you can ask to get together in real life. If and when people say yes, keep in mind that you are working around their schedule, not yours, and you should be traveling to go to a place that's easy for them to get to. Additionally, when you do meet for coffee or even a meal, you should be paying for them. The goal here is to make them remember your real-life interaction as stress-free, engaging, and pleasant as your Reach Out message chain.

///////////////////////

TL; DR: THE GIFT AND THE FAVOR

- In each of your Reach Outs, there will be at least two Gifts (what you are giving someone), and there *might* also be a Favor (what you are asking of someone).

- There is a minimum of at least two Gifts you should offer all the people you Reach Out to—a combo of Gift #1 and any one of Gifts #2 to #5:

  - ◎ **Gift #1:** A compliment, plus one of the following:

  - ◎ **Gift #2:** An article or book recommendation that your Target might like

  - ◎ **Gift #3:** Knowledge you have access to that they don't or something special only you can create

  - ◎ **Gift #4:** A press opportunity

  - ◎ **Gift #5:** Free advice on a skill you have that would benefit them

- The key to a great Favor is to ask a particular, definable question that can't be answered by Googling but can be answered easily via email.

YOUR REACH OUT STRATEGY PLAN

Chose five of your top Targets from the brainstormed list you wrote down in the Chapter 3 prompt. Under each

(Continues)

Target, write down at least two Gifts you could provide for each of them and, if needed, one Favor you could ask from each of them. If you can't think of unique Gifts to give or Favor to ask of them, choose a different Target in their place. This question of "Do I have a unique Gift and/or a Favor to ask of them?" will help cut down the long list of brainstormed Targets created in Chapter 3's prompt. Once you have five Targets with Gifts and/or Favors for each, these are your first week's Reach Outs.

THE FOUR MAIN TYPES OF ROs

Your current connection to the Target tells you what kind of Reach Out you are sending. There are four main different types of Reach Outs (ROs) that all Reach Out messages fall into:

1. **The Re-RO:** Reaching Out to someone you already know from the past or someone you know currently but not well

2. **The Follow-Up RO:** Reaching Out to someone you have met recently in passing in real life

3. **The Borrowed Connection RO:** Reaching Out to a friend of a friend or being introduced by someone who has suggested you two should know each other

4. **The Cool RO:** Reaching Out to someone with whom you have no direct connection

Let's talk about what you can expect when starting to Reach Out to your own Targets.

FIRST, WHAT IS REASONABLE
FOR RO RESPONSE RATES?

It's a huge myth that if you are "good at networking," you'll get a response 100 percent of the time you Reach Out to someone. Even someone well known and with a recognizable name doesn't get that kind of perfect response rate. To keep from feeling discouraged about how often a Target responds to your Reach Outs, especially when starting out, let's talk about what's reasonable to expect. (*Note:* These numbers are based on my own Reaching Out over years of consistent Reach Outs—but of course, they probably will vary slightly for your particular inbox.)

- Re-RO

  - Response rate: ~80 percent.

  - Someone you already know, no matter how long it's been since you last spoke, tends to have the highest response rate, as the Target recognizes your name.

- Follow-Up RO

  - Response rate: ~60 percent.

  - This is someone you've met very recently offline, so you are at the top of his or her mind.

- Borrowed Connection RO

  - Response rate: Depends heavily on who is the connection you have in common.

◉ The closer or more prestigious the Target thinks the mutual connection is, the higher the response rate is likely to be.

- Cool ROs

  ◉ Response rate: ~25 percent.

  ◉ This person doesn't know who you are and therefore has less drive and urgency to respond to your email.

MIXING IT UP

The chance of response goes down as you travel farther out of your network, so using a mix of Reach Out types is the best course of action. Because Cool ROs tend to have the lowest response rate, they should be no more than 20 percent of your total Reach Outs (so for every workweek, no more than one out of the five). The other types (Re-ROs, Follow-Up ROs, and Borrowed Connection ROs) can be more variable depending on where you are in your career.

When working on market research for Messy Bun, I focus mainly on Re-ROs and Borrowed Connection ROs within the target market of podcast creators, wannabe creators, and listeners. Follow-Up ROs are used for people I've met at events that have information about the start-up space that is valuable to me, and I save the rare Cool RO for potential partners or influential podcasters that I can't find any other connection to. But really, my best success has been with the first three kinds, not the Cool ROs.

You want to focus on the edge of the network, not all the way in left field of your network. Now let's go into the details for each type of RO.

> *Out on the edge you see all kinds of things you can't see from the center. [. . .] Big, undreamed-of things—the people on the edge see them first.*
>
> —KURT VONNEGUT, *PLAYER PIANO*

THE DIFFERENT TYPES OF REACH OUTS

Type 1: The Re-RO

Your first Reach Out should be one that has the highest likelihood of success to encourage you to keep going, and that is usually a Re-RO.

The Re-RO is connecting with people you already have familiarly with, such as a current acquaintance or someone you knew well in the past. A current acquaintance would be a weak tie (we learned about weak ties in Chapter 1), and someone you were close to in the past would be a dormant tie. A dormant tie provides new information the way a weak tie does but has some of the closeness of a strong tie: the best of both worlds.[1]

A Re-RO is a great way to break into Reaching Out because the Targets will recognize your name in their inbox and you usually will already have some way of getting in touch, so it's one less step to get the RO sent.

Alessia Tenebruso started Reaching Out after participating in a Reach Out Initiative (you can learn more about Reach Out Initiatives, which are basically book clubs for Reaching Out, in

Chapter 11). Alessia is a Long Island, New York, entrepreneur who is launching a specialty cake business called Free Spirit Cake Co. She describes herself as "pretty shy when it comes to asking for help." Because of this, Alessia found that it was easier to begin with Re-ROs when first starting to execute a Reach Out Strategy. Her first Reach Out was to someone she went to high school with who had started a brownie business; because they had a shared education history and now both work in the bakery business, the positive response she got to her Re-RO encouraged her to continue Reaching Out.

Examples of Re-ROs, Including Gifts and Favors

- **Target:** Your former intern who has a new full-time job at a cool new firm.

  - **Gift:** A compliment plus asking if she would like to attend an industry conference with you that you have a plus-one to.

  - **Favor:** Would she be willing to share feedback on your management style so you can be a better manager to this year's interns?

- **Target:** An old teacher whose class you still think of often.

  - **Gift:** A compliment plus an article that reminded you of something you learned in his class.

  - **Favor:** Can he give you some advice on whether additional schooling is the right move for you?

- **Target:** Someone who was on an intramural team with you who now works in an industry you'd like to get into.

  - **Gift:** A compliment plus asking if she would like to be interviewed on your podcast.

  - **Favor:** Does she have any tips on what you could do now to position yourself to move into the new industry?

And a just-for-fun Re-RO: On people's actual birthday, their inbox is usually overwhelmed with emailed cards, retail birthday coupons, and more. The day after their birthday, rise to the top of the inbox with a Reach Out wishing them a great first full day of their new year.

Type 2: The Follow-Up RO

The Follow-Up RO is sent to someone you've met recently in real life at an event, and you'd like to solidify the connection. Examples of events to meet a Follow-Up RO Target include career fairs, conferences, networking events, industry brunches, parties, store openings, charity fund-raisers, and countless more. At the event, your interaction with the individual could have ranged from just shaking hands to an in-depth 20-minute conversation that ended with the person saying, "We should get coffee."

To get the contact info of people you directly spoke with, ask for a business card at the end of the conversation. The main rule with business cards is that if you ask for one, you must follow up, regardless of hierarchy of titles. No excuses.

If you don't exchange business cards at the event, try to get enough information about your Targets, such as first name, job, and location, to help you find them on LinkedIn so you can send them a message there. It's best to send a Follow-Up RO as soon as you can after the event so your name and the event are at the top of their minds.

The Follow-Up RO is important here because there is simply no point in making the effort to go to in-person events if you don't follow up. Nobody pitches, accepts, and signs a partnership agreement at a cocktail hour. It's not likely you'll be offered a new job while eating your conference boxed lunch. All the magic happens in the follow-up. Be the person who actually follows up so the magic can happen to you too.

Examples of Follow-Up ROs

- **Target:** At a friend's housewarming party, you struck up a great conversation with someone who, as it turns out, works in the office building next to yours. You've been looking to have some new lunch buddies who can get you out of the office on occasion.

  - **Gift:** A compliment on how much you enjoyed meeting him and a Groupon for the sushi place down the street from both your offices.

  - **Favor:** Does he want to grab lunch together on a summer Friday?

- **Target:** At the company town hall, you end up standing in the back with someone from another team. After introducing yourselves, you realize you are sometimes on the same email chains but have never actually met in person.

- ⊚ **Gift:** A compliment on how nice it was to meet in person and a slide deck your team is working on because you know she'd be interested in the brainstorming process.

- ⊚ **Favor:** Could she send you back one or two suggestions to improve the deck that your team hasn't thought of yet?

- **Target:** The person sitting next to you at a conference struck up a conversation with you about how much he admired the speaker.

  - ⊚ **Gift:** A compliment on how much you enjoyed his conversation and an article in which the speaker was quoted or published that you think he hasn't seen before.

  - ⊚ **Favor:** What other industry conferences does he attend that are worthwhile?

A Follow-Up RO can also be done using social media—even Snapchat. Lane Sutton, a Boston-based marketing and employer brand strategist, shares how he uses Snapchat to Reach Out:

I attended a conference in San Francisco this January. Instead of exchanging business cards and email addresses, I added a few people on Snapchat. One of the conference attendees I connected with on Snapchat expressed interest in having me speak at a conference, so we arranged a time to meet. A few weeks later, I was speaking to 600 people at his conference (and I made sure to snap a selfie with the audience).

The Three Hs and the Three Ls: Quick In-Person Networking Tips

Having a structure for how to talk to new people tends to lower anxiety, so here is my basic three-H (*H*i, *H*ow are you, *H*ost) outline to use when leading off an in-person conversation with someone new at an event:

- "*H*i, I'm _____!" (Shake hands; the person will introduce himself or herself too.)

- "*H*ow are you?" (The person will most likely say something nondescript, like "Good," or make some sort of funny joke, like "Fighting my way through the crowds for a piece of cake." React to what the person said; e.g., "I know! It's packed in here!") Then transition into . . .

- "So where do you know [*H*ost's name] from?" (If the host is a company, ask how the person is familiar with the company; if the host is a conference, ask why the person is attending; if the host is a person, ask how the two know each other.)

From there, you will be off and running in a conversation with someone new. At this point, just remember the three Ls: be *L*ighthearted, *L*isten to what people are saying, and try to keep them *L*aughing.

Some other in-person networking tips:

- Practice answers to common small talk questions before walking into the event. Popular small talk questions include "What do you do?," "What industry are you in?," "How long have you lived here?," and "How did you get involved in this cause/organization?"

- If you are going to an event, such as a high school reunion, where people will want to see a picture of your significant other/children/cool vacation, make the image your home screen on your phone so you can easily show the photo without having to flip through your other photos.

- If the idea of going to events alone still makes you nervous, plan to meet a friend at some point during an event, preferably not at the start. This gives you the experience of walking into an event and spending a few minutes talking to new people alone, but it will also give you a level of comfort in knowing that your friend will be joining you soon.

Type 3: The Borrowed Connection RO

The Borrowed Connection RO is the classic "friend of a friend" introduction, also known as a "warm intro." This is when you ask friends or acquaintances to connect you to someone in their network you want to know or when friends or acquaintances offer to connect you to someone they know but you don't.

It can feel more vulnerable to Reach Out to someone with whom you have a friend in common because you're afraid that the Target will feel a weird sense of obligation to help you because of your mutual connection even if the person doesn't want to. I understand that fear, but I also think Borrowed Connection ROs are one of the best ways to show *yourself* what expanding your network can do: it helps you realize you can tap into all these secondary connections and makes your community feel larger, instantly.

When your mutual contact gives you someone's email to Reach Out to directly, double-check that your contact has confirmed with the Target that it was OK to share the email. Once that is confirmed, call out the connector's name in the subject line to grab the Target's attention. If you are introduced on an email by the connector, reply back to both the Target and the connector, thanking the connector for the introduction and explaining that you have moved the connector to BCC to save his or her inbox from overcrowding, and then go right into your Reach Out email to the Target.

Examples of Borrowed Connection ROs

- **Target:** Your roommate's cousin just graduated from the grad school you want to attend.

  - **Gift:** Compliment the cousin on getting into such an awesome grad school program (it must be, if you want to go) and send her an article related to the field you both are interested in.

  - **Favor:** What's the most unexpected thing about this particular grad school program that you couldn't learn from the admissions website?

- **Target:** Your parents' friend's son is more senior to you in your industry and would be a great mentor for you

  - ⊚ **Gift:** Compliment him on something specific his company is doing that is forward-thinking and excites you (remember, Google alerts can help here) and offer him an opportunity to be featured on your industry blog.

  - ⊚ **Favor:** You've began to start thinking about your next career move, and unsure what type of role would best help you end up with where you want to be in five years. Does he have any suggestions on next steps? (As we will see in the next chapter, you don't ask someone to be your mentor right off the bat—you build a relationship with the person first, and mentorship unfolds over time.)

- **Target:** You've moved to a new city, and a friend recommends you Reach Out to her old coworker who lives there too and, like you, also loves jazz.

  - ⊚ **Gift:** A compliment that your mutual friend said about the coworker (such as "Taylor says you're the smartest coworker she's ever had" or "Annie can't stop raving at how well you balance a busy job and your side hustle") and an article about the best jazz spots in your new city.

  - ⊚ **Favor:** Usually, for a Borrowed Connection RO that is more friendship based than career based, the Favor will be getting together in person. The person who connected you both is vouching for each of you, and getting together in person is a nice next step for the budding friendship. Offer coffee to start (maybe at a place that has live jazz music during brunch) and, as always, also offer to meet the person at a place convenient for her.

Borrowed Connection ROs are unique in that they help strengthen your relationship with the connector too. To thank the connector, send two emails: one right after the connection is made to thank the connector for the connection and the other after you've communicated with the Target to let the connector know what became of the connection. You'll want to focus on the positives here; even if the friend of the connector didn't offer to pass along your résumé or didn't have an interest in getting coffee, letting the connector know that the friend is smart/knowledgeable/awesome is a way both to compliment the Target and backhandedly to compliment the connector for knowing a cool person. (If the connector's friend never responded to your email, then you only need to send the connector one email: a "Thank you for connecting us" email. And sometimes this happens. Just because the connector is vouching for you doesn't mean that the Target will write back—it's a contact, not a contract.)

The Borrowed Connection RO is a great way to expand your network organically through secondary connections and has a much higher success rate over the Cool RO, which is the next level down in terms of Reach Out response rates.

Type 4: The Cool RO

The Cool RO is for when you don't know the Target at all and can't find anyone in your network who does, either. This is a long-shot RO and a bit of a last resort. Because it's a long shot, only 20 percent or less of your Reach Outs should be Cool ROs, and you should try your best to connect with the Target through the other RO types before resorting to this cold approach.

With Cool ROs, it's important to keep in mind that the bigger the fish, the lower the chance of a response. Is it cool to send an email to someone famous and get a response? Yes! But is it likely that someone famous will have the time to help you? Probably not. If the CEO of J.Crew responds to your email giving you advice on how to break into fashion, that's awesome. But the head of your local boutique could give you similarly valuable advice and might also have the time and space to offer to let you shadow or intern at their store. So try to focus less on "famous" people and more on people who might actually have the time and likelihood of helping you.

With that in mind, take a critical eye to the list of potential Targets you've created in Chapter 3. Cross off the names of people who are not easy to contact or will to be too busy to return an email. (Here, I'll help: Take off Taylor Swift and any member of the Obama family other than Bo the dog.)

If you want to break into sending Cool ROs, a great first one is Reaching Out to an author. Think of the last book you read and enjoyed, and hunt around a bit until you find the author's contact information online. Send a quick email expressing your thanks for writing something that made you think/happy/laugh/feel less alone, etc. Authors hope that readers will connect with their books, so this is a Cool RO that is usually very well received.

Another type of Cool RO that is usually well received is one where, after reading an article (whether in the *New York Times* or in a small industry blog), you Reach Out to someone mentioned or quoted who catches your eye and let that person know you are impressed by what you read. By showing you are reading the type of publication the person is being featured in, you subtly suggest that you two are running in similar circles.

PEEK INTO THE INBOX OF:

A Famous Author

I Am: Cody Miles, creative director of Brandcave

The Target: Andy Weir, author of *The Martian*

The RO Type: Cool RO

The Backstory: In a moment of desperation, I Reached Out to Andy Weir, author of *The Martian*, the book that was made into a film in 2015 starring Matt Damon. I had been producing a marketing campaign for an unknown author who was demanding high returns in the first month of his debut book's release. It had been a rough month trying to meet his insanely high expectations and I had been unsuccessful at every attempt. It was so bad that I would have nightmares about future meetings. I even considered changing careers. At the time, I was also reading *The Martian* and it occurred to me: How did this relatively obscure science fiction author produce a top-selling debut novel? How did that novel turn into a film so quickly? So, in a moment of "what the hell else do I do?," I emailed Andy Weir.

The Subject Line: Looking for Advice

The Reach Out Email:

> Hi Andy,
>
> I hope you're doing great. My name is Cody. I know you're extremely busy but I was wondering if I could pick your brain for no more than twenty minutes. I'm trying to help a client of mine promote his book with little success. The pressure is enormous and I feel as though I've hit rock bottom. Every tactic I know has been exhausted.
>
> I don't expect you'll have all the answers but it would be helpful to hear from you, however brief our conversation might be. Would you consider scheduling a call with me? Or perhaps answering a few questions by email?
>
> Thank you for your consideration. Thanks for writing *The Martian* too. I thoroughly enjoyed it.
>
> Cody

The Response Time: 1 day

The Outcome: Andy convinced me that I wasn't a bad marketer. He told me that he had actually spent the last 10 years building a list of subscribers to his blog. By the time he was ready to release *The Martian*, he already had 3,000 buyers ready to go. He gave me a few other hints and said under no uncertain terms, to drop the client. So, I did. Thanks Andy!

Five Ways to Find a Target's Contact Info

For Cool ROs, it can be hard to find a Target's contact information. Here are some ideas on how to contact people you don't know and have no connections to:

1. Look for their personal website; this usually has either an email or a contact form. Googling their name/job title/company usually does the trick here.

2. If you're coming up short, move on to LinkedIn, typing in their job title or company name to narrow down the search. Once you've found them on LinkedIn, you can request to join their network with a personalized message.

3. Still no luck? Try Twitter and see if they list an email address on their profiles. If they follow you, you can direct-message them. Rasheen Carbin, the cofounder of job search app nspHire, shares another great way to find someone's email address:

   > I use a site called AllMyTweets (allmytweets.net/connect). Enter the Target's Twitter handle in the search bar. This will bring up a chronological list of their tweets. Next, use Ctrl + F to bring up a search box. Type "email," "email address," or, even better, the probable domain name of the Target. This may bring up several matches; you will be able to see if they've ever tweeted out their email address.

4. If none of the above works, it's time to take more advanced steps. If the Target sends out a newsletter, get on that list.

It makes it easy to stay up-to-date on what the person is doing, and if you click "Reply," sometimes you'll end up right in the Target's personal inbox. Carrie Aulenbacher, a romance writer in Erie, Pennsylvania, did just this by responding to the newsletter that Dani Collins, a Harlequin Presents writer, regularly sends to her fans and readers. Carrie wrote an encouraging note after Dani mentioned something that was getting her down in the newsletter. The exchange sparked a months-long email chain about the romance novel industry, with the two writers sharing advice and encouragement with each other, even though they are at different stages of their careers.

5. And finally, if you hit dead ends with all these steps, it might be time to take it offline. Kate Pratt, director of team sales and marketing partnerships at The Madison Square Garden Company, suggests:

> If you cannot find an e-mail address, but know where the person you are Reaching Out to works, look up their company address and mail a thoughtful, short note with your business card. In this high-tech world, it is important to diversify yourself. I find, at times, breaking through can be as simple as sending a handwritten letter to cut through the clutter of electronic mail.

If you use this technique, send only one letter through snail mail. More than one can come off as invasive in a way that multiple emails do not.

POP QUIZ!

Q: What kind of RO is Reaching Out to your favorite blogger that you have never met before and have no mutual connections to?
A: That is a Cool RO—you have no prior connection to them.

Q: What kind of RO is Reaching Out to someone in your field whom you sat next to at a friend's birthday party last weekend?
A: That is a Follow-Up RO—you have met briefly and want to build a deeper connection.

Q: What kind of RO is being introduced over email to your uncle's best friend who might be a potential investor in your new business?
A: That is a Borrowed Connection RO, as you have a mutual contact that put you in touch.

Q: What kind of RO is Reaching Out to your old boss whom you have lost touch with?
A: That is a Re-RO, as this person is someone you used to know well.

////////////////////

TL; DR: THE FOUR MAIN TYPES OF ROS

- There are four main types of ROs:

  1. **The Re-RO:** Reaching Out to someone you knew in the past or someone you know currently, but not well. Starting with a Re-RO, which usually has the highest

response rate, is a great way to jump into Reaching Out as you will usually be encouraged by your positive response to keep going.

2. **The Follow-Up RO:** Reaching Out to someone you have met in passing offline recently.

3. **The Borrowed Connection RO:** Reaching Out to a friend of a friend or being introduced by someone who has suggested you two should know each other.

4. **The Cool RO:** Reaching Out to someone with whom you have no direct connection.

- The chance of response goes down as you travel further out of your network. Re-ROs have the highest chance of a response, and Cool ROs have the lowest.

- Cool ROs should be no more than 20 percent of your total Reach Outs, as they are the least likely to get a response and therefore are not a great use of your time compared with the other three RO types.

YOUR REACH OUT STRATEGY PLAN

Mark each of the five Targets you've identified as your first week's Reach Outs as being a Re-RO, Follow-Up RO, Borrowed Connection RO, or Cool RO. Remember, no more than one of five should be a Cool RO. Then find each Target's contact information and put it into your plan.

REACHING OUT TO MEET YOUR GOALS

O ne of my happiest memories is being a 10-year-old on New Year's Eve. I went to a party with my parents and younger sister, and we must have left before midnight because I remember being in my childhood bedroom with a cup of sparkling apple cider writing out my New Year's resolutions into my Lisa Frank diary as the clock turned from one year into the next. There is just something so hopeful and optimistic about setting new goals. No matter your age or the date on the calendar, a fresh goal makes any day feel new.

If you picked up this book, I can safely assume you're either (1) a goal-oriented person who wants to get ahead or (2) someone who wants to become more goal oriented to get ahead.

Here are specific strategies on how to use the four different kinds of ROs to reach the career goals you developed in Chapter 3 from your Love/Don't Love list, whether your goals are to find a new job, get promoted, gain more responsibility within your current company, expand your business, get press coverage, make friends, or find a mentor. Feel free to skip to the section(s) that most aligns with your current or future goals.

REACHING OUT TO FIND A NEW JOB

When you tell people you want a new job, whether it's your first job out of school or your fifth, the first piece of advice you are often given is "network!"

But as we've already learned, a network is people you know, not something you do. When people say that you need to "network" to find a new role, what they really mean is that by reminding your weak ties about your skills and what you're looking for *and* by putting yourself out there to meet new people, you'll be more likely to come across interesting job opportunities you wouldn't have known about otherwise. Here are the particular ways you can use each type of RO to help you land a new role:

The Notecard Method

The Notecard Method is a job search method that can help take some of the pressure off the process. All you have to do is make a check mark on a notecard whenever you apply for a job, with the goal being to get to 100 check marks, equivalent to 100 job applications.

I made up the Notecard Method when I was feeling discouraged by a hard job search a few years ago. By putting check marks on the card each day, I felt like I was making progress instead of overfocusing on how much pressure I felt to "get a new job, like, right now." By focusing on something within my control (applying to jobs) rather than out of my control (landing the job, which is the whim of hiring managers, company timelines, and more), I was able to keep my morale up.

If you follow the Notecard Method, you'll probably get a job before you hit 100 check marks. I think I accepted a job around check mark 60 or so—but it helped enormously with keeping me motivated. Baby steps are still steps! Try it if you're in a similar space in your life.

- **Re-RO:** Reaching Out to someone you know from your past or someone you currently know loosely to land a job can be *extremely* effective. Remember how we talked in Chapter 1 about weak ties being more valuable than strong ties in the job hunt? This is where you see that take shape.

  A strong Re-RO is to a former coworker you know enjoyed working with you, whether you or your ex-coworker left the company; people tend to feel an affinity toward helping people they used to work with. Even if the Target doesn't work at the exact kind of company you want to work at, he or she might know of an opening elsewhere to pass along.

  Another type of Re-RO that can be useful when working to land a new role is to Reach Out to someone who interviewed you before but passed you over for that role at that time. Wait until at least six months has elapsed, and

Reach Out with any updates or highlights that have happened in your professional life since your interview. Be sure to throw in a bit of info that shows you've been following the company recently too, whether it's referencing a news story or an industry trend that has affected the company since you interviewed. End the Reach Out by saying how interested you remain in working at the company and calling out any new jobs listed on the site that you are qualified for.

- **Follow-Up RO:** If you're actively on the job hunt, you are possibly attending networking events. And if you're transitioning to a new field, you're probably starting to attend events and conferences in this new-to-you industry. If so, be strategic about the people you speak to at the event and be dedicated about following up with them or other speakers after. If you are attending a networking event hosted by a specific group, you can typically email the administrator of the group and ask for a list of people who have registered so far; the administrator might not always send it, but it's worth a shot. The administrator may also send a list of the companies with employees attending rather than individual names, which can still be helpful. Do research and have two or three specific people in mind whom you want to connect with at the event. Then, when you meet them at the event, ask for a business card to follow up. If you don't get a business card, you can find and probably connect with them on LinkedIn after, with a short message reminding them where you met.

When chatting at the event, remember the basic three-H (*H*i, *H*ow are you, *H*ost) outline as well as the three Ls (be *L*ighthearted, *L*isten to what they are saying, and try to keep them *L*aughing) from Chapter 5. If the conversation is going well, you can mention you're actively looking for a job. If the conversation stays more in the "small talk" realm, use the Follow-Up RO to work your job search goals into the conversation. Here you can ask about a specific job you see on their company's careers page or just let them know you're actively looking in the field of X in case they know of any roles that would fit the bill.

- **Borrowed Connection RO:** The Borrowed Connection RO is why it's important to always be talking to others about what kind of job you'd like or the type of field you want to learn more about, even at noncareer or nonofficial networking events. Whether at your neighbor's BBQ or friend's girlfriend's birthday party, when someone hears what you are interested in and suggests, "Oh, you might need to know X," be joyful and enthusiastic and ask to be connected.

  Former bosses or coworkers can also be great sources for Borrowed Connection ROs because they can validate to others what a talented employee you are. Irnande Altema, an attorney in the state of Maryland and the founder of FirstGenRise, went to law school because of her aspirations to work for a senator. When she returned home to Maryland after graduating law school in New York, she Reached Out to her former boss whom she had worked with prior to law school. She shared her interest in working in government relations or legislative affairs, and because he knew she did great work, he connected her to a legislative consultant. From this Borrowed Connection RO, Irnande had a meeting with the consultant that led to a job offer at his firm. This Reach Out kick-started her law career and led to her connecting with Maryland State Senator Kathy Klausmeier, for whom she is now chief legislative counsel.

- **Cool RO:** This RO is the key for Reaching Out to human resources (HR) professionals, in-house recruiters, or hiring managers at companies you'd like to work at.

   I was talking to a friend of mine who works in HR at a big consulting firm, and she explained that prospective hires often Reach Out via LinkedIn asking what jobs are open that they would be qualified for. This is a huge bummer for her. All open roles are listed on the firm's website, and it's not someone else's job to match you with a job (with the exception of outside search firms). It's your job to find a job you're qualified for and sell either HR or the hiring manager on why you should be interviewed for it. Reaching Out to someone in HR asking what jobs you are qualified for is a quick way to look like an amateur.

   It's best to save the Cool RO to HR either until there is an actual job you're interested in and are qualified for or if you have specific questions whose answers you are *sure* are not available on the Internet. If you're Reaching Out for a specific job, make sure the job is reasonable for you to apply for, but keep in mind you only need to have 50 percent or more of the job qualifications before you apply. Most people wait to apply until they have 110 percent of the qualifications listed, and this is a mistake. A list of qualifications is usually a wish list put together by the employer, not a must-have list. You don't want to be overqualified for the job you're applying for—your next position should grow and challenge you, not already be something you can do in your sleep.

Besides a company's website, you can also use one of the following sites to find an open job:

- angel.co/jobs

- glassdoor.com/job

- idealist.org

- indeed.com

- jobs.mashable.com

- linkedin.com/jobs

- mediabistro.com/joblistings

- monster.com

- planted.com

- remote.co

- saywerk.com

- simplyhired.com

- themuse.com/jobs

After you see an open job you're qualified for (remember, you only need 50 percent of the qualifications), head over to LinkedIn to see who you know at the company who could help you as a Re-RO or a Borrowed Connection RO (using the first and second connections filter and searching by company name will be helpful here). If you don't have any connection, start looking to see who could be a Target of a Cool RO; most likely it will be either the probable hiring manager for the job or, at a larger company, an in-house recruiter.

If you initiate any type of RO related to a job search and the Target responds, it is good karma not only to thank the Target but also to circle back and report what happened with the opportunity down the road, even if you didn't get the job. This is true even if you abandon your search after you start Reaching Out. Maybe you decide not to switch jobs, not to change cities, etc. Either way, you have initiated a Reach Out and a person took the time to help you, so it is courteous to let the person know your status and how much the help meant to you (even if it was really only a bit of help). A simple "Just wanted to update you that I took myself out of the job search process after I got a promotion in my current role. Thank you so much for your willingness to help me and the insights you shared with me. I hope we can stay in touch" is all it takes. This also keeps the door open for a Re-RO when you might need help again—or the person might need yours.

The big secret in life is that there is no big secret.
Whatever your goal for this year is, you can get there—
as long as you're willing to be honest with yourself
about the preparation and work involved.
—Oprah Winfrey, "What I Know for Sure"[1]

REACHING OUT TO GET PROMOTED OR TO GET MORE RESPONSIBILITY AT YOUR CURRENT COMPANY

Reaching Out can also help advance your career at your *current* job. To do this, you'll need your colleagues to be aware of who you are, what you're working on, and what you're good at. By staying on the radar of as many coworkers as possible via Reaching Out, you are more likely to be considered for special projects and to be seen as an expert by other departments, both of which can lead to a formal promotion or raise.

- **Re-RO:** Is there someone you worked with on a project a few quarters ago but have lost touch with? Send a note (maybe with an inside joke or funny memory from the project) and ask what the person is working on these days that you could help with.

- **Follow-Up RO:** Sit next to someone new at a meeting? Introduce yourself and ask about the person's role. It should be easy to find contact info in the company email system, so follow up with a note and an article related to the meeting to continue the conversation or ask the person to join you for lunch in the cafeteria or coffee at the place around the corner. (I usually think asking someone for an in-person meeting is a bit much for an initial Reach Out, but since you work in the same building and are employed by the same company, it's OK here.)

- **Borrowed Connection RO:** When your boss says, "Do you know Monique in finance?" respond with a simple, "No, not yet, but I'd love to meet her and hear her thoughts on X. Could you introduce us?" Showing this kind of initiative will impress your boss and coworkers while also allowing you to meet new contacts at work. Both the Follow-Up RO and the Borrowed Connection RO can be key to finding a sponsor, internal mentor, or new work BFF.

- **Cool RO:** Working at a huge company with an interoffice directory is great when it comes to the Cool RO. Think strategically about other groups you'd love to partner with on projects or internal people you'd love to work for someday. Send your Targets a message with a genuine compliment on their team's work and an article they might find interesting. Then, if they work in your office location, ask if they have time to tell you more about their role in hopes of finding some synergies (office speak!) between your two groups. Show up to the meeting with questions about their work and some ideas in your head of how your two groups could work together (and maybe some doughnuts or other treats), and you're on your way to making a stronger connection with colleagues as well as raising your workplace profile and influence. Feel free to invite another member of your team along as well for maximum brainstorming.

Looking for another way to use networking to get ahead at your current role? Be open and generous about connecting coworkers to those in your network *outside* of the company. People who seem well connected look like better fits for management because it is assumed their larger network can benefit the company.

REACHING OUT TO INCREASE SALES OR EXPAND YOUR BUSINESS

If you're a business owner, you're probably hyperfocused on how to increase your clients or sales. This is true whether you are a one-person Etsy shop or a business that makes millions each year. To ensure you're attracting the right kind of new customers, let's break down how to use each type of RO:

- **Re-RO:** This is as simple as Reaching Out to past (happy) clients and asking them if they are interested in your services again or in a new product you are offering. Take into account your business cycle—if the work you provide is seasonal, on a subscription basis, or if access expires, aim to ask 7 to 60 days before their current contract ends. The more expensive the item, the earlier you should ask them if they would like to renew or the sooner you should offer an upsell.

- **Follow-Up RO:** You'll want to attend events with your target market, not events just for entrepreneurs or business owners. If you sell mainly to pet owners, start going to local dog Meetup groups with samples and business cards, not just attending conferences indoors with other business owners.

- **Borrowed Connection RO:** Referrals are one of the easiest ways to expand your business without spending tons of additional marketing dollars to capture new customers. Offering a referral bonus, or even just a thoughtful, personalized note expressing your deep gratitude to the connector for sending a new customer your way, can help send more sales from secondary connections your way.

- **Cool RO:** Approaching potential clients cold is tough. Methods such as buying email lists or going through your Instagram followers looking for potential customers can be fruitless in most industries. Because the Cool RO can be tough to use to land new customers unless you are in an incredibly niche field, there are three hints to make your digital profile look open to letting the right kind of customers find *you*: (1) add text to your social media profiles that explains your business, with links to your website or favorite product offerings; (2) have clear "click-to-buy" links, a contact number, or live chat with a customer service rep on your blog, website, and/or social media; and (3) highlight what you want to be known for and the type of customer you want to attract. For example, even if the bulk of your company's revenue is doing B2C sales, if you want to do more B2B sales, highlight the B2B offerings on your website via testimonials, images, and service offerings.

REACHING OUT FOR PRESS COVERAGE

The rise of personal branding means that many more people pitch themselves for personal press coverage directly to journalists. While large companies or celebrities might have an entire PR team that handles their press coverage, most individuals do their own PR, at least when they are starting out. Some common examples of press coverage to help with an individual's personal brand include being quoted or mentioned in an article and being interviewed on a blog, podcast, or video. The reason individuals would want press coverage is to help brand themselves and solidify their influence as an expert in a certain space. The techniques below work in building your own personal press coverage, but they also work well for landing coverage for your company. I often use the Re-RO or the Cool RO when pitching to get coverage for Messy Bun.

- **Re-RO:** If you've received press in a publication before, Reaching Out to the publication to run a follow-up story or to offer a quote as an expert for a new story can work well. Try to let at least six months go by before pitching a new story idea to the reporter, and have a new angle (for example, new products, new features, a new job, or a milestone you just hit would all be valid reasons to Reach Out).

- **Follow-Up RO:** If you're attending events with journalists, bloggers, or podcasters, follow up with those you've met in person by offering to give a quote or be an interview subject for any upcoming pieces they might be working on. Keep in mind that press cycles can be long, especially if the topic is not time sensitive, so you might not hear back right away. Don't get discouraged: focus on building the relationship with the writer rather than getting an immediate press hit.

- **Borrowed Connection RO:** This one can be tricky because not all journalists like to share contacts. But if the journalist, podcaster, or blogger seems open to it, you could ask if there is anyone else in the industry you should meet. Media that cover one space often have a lot of contacts in that specific industry, so if you're in tech and talking to a tech writer, asking for suggestions of anyone who would be good for you to know in the space (press or not) might lead the tech writer to offer to do an introduction.

- **Cool RO:** For press coverage, a Cool RO means general pitching to journalists you have no relationship to and encouraging them to write about your story idea. A pitch email isn't a pure Reach Out, but it's something most people looking to increase their press clippings often want to know about, so I'm including it here. The key in a pitch email is to keep it short and sweet and not too formal. People get tons of impersonal emails every day. Your emails are from a real person—you!—and they should be written as such.

David Tabor, a digital content marketer at Joosr, echoes this thought, saying, "We feel our success pitching for press coverage from publications or influencers is a result of keeping emails light and quick. We've tried several methods, and formal ones often put busy people off, while chatty or friendly ones are well received." Try to phrase these Cool ROs as if you were emailing with a friend. *Rule of thumb:* If you don't say "Kind regards" in text messages to friends, don't say it in a Reach Out.

Another key point is not to pitch publications via a blind email—always find a specific reporter to pitch. You can find writers to pitch by searching a publication's masthead or by searching on Twitter or LinkedIn. You're more likely to get a response by pitching a person rather than a blind email inbox. Here's a template of how to pitch a reporter for press coverage:

Hi [name],

I've been following your work at [publication or platform's name(s)] for a while, and I've especially loved [reference two or more pieces that came out two-plus months ago to show longtime following]. I know you write/speak/care a lot about [topic], and I have a story idea that I think might fall into your wheelhouse. [Two sentences about the idea you are pitching.]

I'd love to provide an interview or quote about [three things you can talk about], or [if you run or work for a business you're looking to receive press] I can connect you to any members of our community who can speak about their experiences using our product [name-drop any impressive stories or users].

Thanks for your consideration [name], and I'll continue being a fan of your work,

[your name]

You'll notice here that the Gift is a compliment on their work. Members of the media you'll be pitching each write or produce hundreds of stories, blog posts, podcasts, or videos, and it just looks lazy to reference their most recent work. Instead, mention two to three previous pieces from a few months ago to show you've been following the person's work for a while. The Favor in the template above is asking for press coverage, but you're disguising it as a Gift by giving suggestions for future stories or ideas you can provide expert opinion or coverage on.

Another resource for press coverage that both individuals and companies can use is HARO (helpareporter.com). It's a free resource that matches journalists looking for interview subjects or quotes for stories with people or companies looking for press. As someone looking for press, you sign up for free to receive HARO emails tailored to the subject categories you can speak about. When you see that an outlet is looking for a quote for a story that you can potentially help with, you reply to the email address provided. If the outlet chooses you, that's great free press.

A Carefully Tailored Pitch Email

I Am: Jackson Carpenter, the head of PR for Lucid Software in Utah's Silicon Slopes

The Target: Josh Steimle, a popular marketing thought leader and contributor to sites like Inc., Forbes, and Mashable

RO Type: Cool RO

The Backstory: Josh lives in China, but is from Utah and is very well connected in Utah's tech scene. I wanted him to cover some of my company's recent marketing wins to help us build our reputation locally and grow our recruiting efforts.

The Subject Line: Josh, I took your advice

The Reach Out Email:

Josh,

You suggested that if someone wanted you to write about their company, they might mention that they also went to BYU. That's me! I'm a part-time BYU student and full-time PR head for Lucid Software, a startup based in South Jordan, Utah.

I have a story for you that every marketer can learn something from.

Lucid makes diagramming software (yawn), and needed a way to make itself sexy and interesting to the masses (and the media), so the team started making pop culture flowcharts that have since been featured in The Huffington Post, Gizmodo, ScreenRant, and more. The campaign has won awards and produced over 2 million views for Lucid Software in seven months.

We learned a few things in the process that could be useful to your readers. Per your instructions, here is a <u>link</u> to a rough draft for you to check out.

I know you're a busy guy with a lot on your plate, but I hope to hear back from you nonetheless.

Cheers,

Jackson

The Response Time: 13 days

The Outcome: I let a lot of time pass between follow-ups because that's what Josh said he liked on his website. That meant that it took a little longer to get results, but about a month after our first contact, Josh published the story I pitched him on entrepreneur.com. He also shared the story on his social networks, thereby introducing us to some of the top talent in our market.

REACHING OUT TO MAKE FRIENDS

Even though most of this book is about Reaching Out to get ahead in your professional network, I want to briefly touch on using Reach Out Strategy to make or strengthen your social network.

While I was writing this book, I took a girls' weekend with three friends of mine. As we chatted about Reaching Out, we realized that all four of us had met each other through Reach Outs, primarily through Borrowed Connection and Cool ROs. Reaching Out *can* lead to friendship, but it feels awkward to send an email asking if someone wants to be your friend (*so very awkward*).

There's no tried and true format for making a friend via Reaching Out. I've probably had coffee with more than 100 people in the last few years, and only about 8 of them are now close friends. Reaching Out is always a numbers game, but even more so when you want to build lasting friendships with people.

Reaching Out to make friends is one of the only kinds of ROs in which it makes sense in your first email to ask to get together in person, as friendships are born out of face-to-face interactions, not over email. With a Re-RO, you can ask to have a meal right off the bat. With the other types of ROs, asking for a smaller Favor than a meal (such as coffee or drinks) can be a good first step.

- **Re-RO:** Are there those in your network you used to be closer to, but because of time, distance, or just general life, you stopped seeing them as often? High school or college friends often fall into that category. A simple "Hey, I miss you! I'd love to get together and catch up" is all it can take to start reaching out to old friends.

- **Follow-Up RO:** Did you meet someone at a social event and hit it off? It can feel awkward to ask for someone's number on the spot, but friending the person on social media and then sending a message asking to get together is a nice way to start.

- **Borrowed Connection RO:** This type of RO works great if you are changing cities. Put up a post on whatever social network you are most active on, letting people know you are moving, and ask them to tag people in the comments or introduce you over email to new potential friends in your new location. Then follow up with each person tagged, introducing yourself and asking if you can take the person out to his or her favorite coffee spot in your new hometown to get to know the person better.

- **Cool RO:** The Cool RO can be tougher to make new friends with because you have had no prior relationship or friends who can vouch for you, but sometimes it works if you have the same very specific interests. Sarah Von Bargen, blogger and writer at Yesandyes.org, shares this tale of how she made a new friend with the Cool RO by pointing out their shared commonalities:

> A blogger I'd been reading for years had just returned from a trekking trip to Nepal and was struggling

to re-acclimate to "normal" life. I'd been through the exact same thing two years prior. I Reached Out to her, just to basically say, "I've been there. It sucks. I'm sorry. For what it's worth, I also miss eating momos and curry for every meal." Now we're great friends. We've met up in real life several times and have even gone on vacation together!

I was smart enough to go through any door that opened.
—JOAN RIVERS[2]

REACHING OUT TO GET A MENTOR

Mentoring is about forming a relationship naturally over time. Too often, firms will try to formalize things and create a forced scheduled mentor relationship like, "You will meet with this person twice a month, on these dates, forever and ever." But real mentorship is about having a genuine connection with someone and being able to ask for advice as you need it, not on a specific schedule. A relationship can evolve into a mentorship if you had repeated positive contact over time, and a mentor can be either someone within your current company or someone external (ideally you would have at least one of each). Mentors tend to give advice on overarching career issues and questions that don't necessarily have one right answer.

A mentor relationship evolves over time, so you shouldn't ask someone to be your mentor in your first email. Over time, if a relationship develops, you will naturally start to think of the person as your mentor and even start introducing the person to others or referring to him or her as your mentor—but it's awkward to ask someone to be your mentor right off the bat before you've let an organic relationship develop.

- **Re-RO:** Think back to people you've worked with in the past whom you admired. Old bosses you got along with well are great Re-ROs when you're on the mentor hunt. Treat the Reach Outs in a casual, friendly way by starting with what is going on in their life. Then, after a connection has been reestablished, ask for advice on a challenge or problem you're currently facing at work. People are almost always flattered to be asked for advice, and it will help open up a mentorlike dialogue with them.

- **Follow-Up RO:** Being strategic about the events you attend can help you make connections in person for potential mentors. An amazing person I mentor is Vivian Nunez; Vivian is a talented digital content producer, the founder of Toodamnyoung.com, and a gifted public speaker. Vivian and I connected after she sent me a short message after we spoke briefly at an event, asking me for advice on starting an online brand. Over time, that first question she asked evolved into a mentorship.

    Vivian shared her thought process of being strategic about the events she attended before she Reached Out to me:

    > I deliberately chose to sit in on the Social Media Week 7x7 Mentoring Panel because you were on it, which looking back could be deemed as borderline

creepy, but should actually be seen as flattering. I don't remember the first time I came across Smart, Pretty, & Awkward, but I'd somehow become an adamant follower on Twitter and I was impressed by how you'd built up a community around it. You had the qualities I wanted to develop in myself post-college and having just turned 21 and being three months away from graduation, I didn't want to leave it up to chance that I would one day develop them. I also had a set idea in mind that I wanted your opinion on. Sitting in on the panel was my first step toward figuring out if you would be open to sitting down for coffee or dinner. For me, at the time, I think it was important to have a bit of background or history develop between us before I Reached Out because I knew I was going to be Reaching Out with a really personal project. I had the beginnings of Too Damn Young (my community and resource for teens and young adults who have lost someone) on paper and it was important to me that I felt like I could trust you and that you wouldn't belittle the idea. I really wanted you to be honest, but it was also important to me that I knew you would be kind. After the one or two seconds we got to speak after the panel, I tweeted you congratulations on doing a great job, then followed that up with a direct message (DM) once you'd responded to the tweet. In the DM, I asked for the best email to reach you on and we started an email chain from there.

Using your time wisely by attending public events where you know potential mentors will be participating helps make what would be a Cool RO turn into a Follow-Up RO. I'm grateful that Vivian has the foresight to see that—I get just as much (actually, probably more) out of our mentoring relationship as she does.

- **Borrowed Connection RO:** Being straightforward and sharing with others that you want to meet more people who can help you with a specific problem in your career can help others think of someone to introduce you to. "I want a mentor to help my career" is too general. Instead, "I'm looking to speak with someone who could help me figure out how to transition from freelance to a full-time role. Do you know anyone?" could help land you an introduction to your new mentor.

- **Cool RO:** This would be extremely similar to emailing someone you don't know (famous or not) and asking for help with a career-related question. After you have a string of positive back-and-forths, if the conversation is still flowing naturally, you can move to the next step of asking the person to do a call, have a video meeting, or get together in person. But, remember that you don't always have to have an offline conversation for someone to be your mentor. Having a thriving back-and-forth email correspondence with someone more experienced in your field means the person is already your mentor whether you have met in person or not.

And Reaching Out is not always about a mentee emailing a potential mentor—sometimes it's the other way around. As Lena Dunham recalled in *The New Yorker* about her mentor, Nora Ephron:

> I devoured her prose, her other film offerings, and became a fangirl right along with my mother, aunt, grandmother, and every other intelligent woman in the tristate area. Which is why it was so momentous when, in March of 2011, I received a short, perfect e-mail from Ephron, saying she had seen and enjoyed my film and would like to take me to lunch."[3]

Nora Reached Out to this potential mentee, not the other way around. This kicked off a wonderful friendship between the two writers that lasted until Nora's passing.

////////////////////

TL; DR: REACHING OUT TO MEET YOUR GOALS

• Most people start Reaching Out because they are interested in changing jobs or starting in a new industry. But Reaching Out isn't just to change roles; it can also be to raise your profile at your current company, increase your business's sales, land press coverage, make friends, or meet your mentor.

YOUR REACH OUT STRATEGY PLAN

Looking at your career goals developed in Chapter 3 from your Love/Don't Love list, take any applicable notes from this chapter and either slightly tweak your Reach Out Strategy Plan to make sure it accurately reflects these goals or write down items to remember and to-dos in your General Notes document as inspiration as you move toward your future.

PART

THE REACH OUT

CHAPTER 7

THE EMAIL TEMPLATE OF YOUR DREAMS

W hen I first starting Reaching Out, I would labor over each email. Now I could write a Reach Out email in my sleep; the template I describe below is second nature. And when I think I've written a particularly good Reach Out email or I receive an email with myself as the Target that catches my eye, I save a copy of it in a Google doc titled "Favorite ROs." That way when I need some inspiration or am a little stuck, I head over there to see if I can gather some ideas. In that doc is also where I save the best one-paragraph description of what Messy Bun is; it serves as an easy reference when I'm emailing Targets about that project.

So if you're feeling stuck on how to actually compose an amazing Reach Out email (which is totally normal), follow Steps One to Eight below—soon you will be able to do this in your sleep, too. As we know from the "Peek into the Inbox of . . ." sections, you don't have to follow this guideline exactly to get a great outcome—but following as much of the basic structure as you can will certainly help. And while I can never guarantee that an email will get a response, from experience I can tell you that if you follow these steps, your chances of getting a response are higher.

And don't worry—I didn't forget about social media Reach Outs. We'll cover those in the next chapter!

CONSTRUCTING YOUR RO EMAIL

Step One: Decide Whether to Send from Your Personal or Work Email

I encourage people to send Reach Outs from their personal, not their work, email. That way if the Target responds to your email later on, even if you've left the company, you will be able to get the email. Also, it is more effective for you to be able to respond to an old email thread, even if it's one you began years ago, when doing a Re-RO because it will help build familiarity and show your history. A personal email address will always be yours to own; a work one will change after you leave the company.

The exception is if you're Reaching Out for something directly related to your job duties. For example, when I worked at Hearst, one of my duties was Reaching Out to popular bloggers for potential partnerships. Since those types of Reach Outs were baked into my job duties, I would send the email from my Hearst email account. To make sure I had a point of contact with the relationships I was building even after I left the company,

I would also connect with the bloggers or their management teams on my LinkedIn.

If your Reach Outs aren't directly related to your job but you work at a well-respected or "cool" company, there is a temptation to use your work email for all your Reach Outs, thinking that the name of your company will catch the other person's eye. I advocate for Reaching Out from your personal email for the reasons outlined above, but there are some work-arounds here:

- Send the initial Reach Out from the work email, and after one email, switch to your personal email.

  - If you are going to use work time or your work email to send Reach Outs that are not directly work related, make sure there is at least some tiny way the Reach Out ties back to your job—you never know who is watching your work computer, and you want to be able to justify it if someone asks.

- Send the email from your work email but CC or BCC your personal email.

- Make your personal email address "display-as" name (something you can change in your email settings) to include the company name, such as "Molly from Buzzfeed" instead of "Molly Beck."

- Include an email signature that calls out your job title and company name on your personal email.

My sister Teri Ford, a senior project engineer who lives in Boston, shares how she thinks about inbox management:

> 90% of the time I Reach Out through my work email because I monitor my work email more closely than my personal email. I don't worry about losing the contact if I left the company because anyone I connect with via email that I have a real relationship with, I would share the news I was leaving the company and ask us to keep in touch. I usually also connect with them on LinkedIn, too.

Step Two: Make Your Subject Line Awesome

Subject lines are especially important if it's a Borrowed Connection or a Cool RO email, because the person won't recognize your name. The three main types of subject lines that are most effective when Reaching Out are:

- Mentioning something specific the Target has created or done:

   ◉ "Inspired by Your June 30 Blog Post"

   ◉ "Was in Audience at Yesterday's Talk"

- Name-dropping a mutual connection:

   ◉ "From Taylor Smith's Friend"

   ◉ "Classmate of Your Wife"

- Mentioning something you and the Target have in common:

  - "I'm a Hamilton-Wenham Regional High School Graduate Too . . . Go Generals!"

  - "Fellow Cleveland Marketer"

Manny Fernandez, the cofounder and CEO of Dream Funded.com, echoes this thought, saying: "I get roughly 1000s of emails a week, probably because of my easy-to-decipher email address of putting my first name and the company together. The emails I respond to first are usually the ones from people that I know or someone who mentions someone I know in the subject line."

You also want to use title case, meaning that every important word in the subject line is capitalized. A study by Yesware's data scientists regarding email subject lines found this to be most effective: "When senders use title case—for example: Subject-Line Story versus subject-line story—emails had a higher open and reply rate. Title case had an open rate of 54.3%, while lower-case subject lines dropped to 47.6%. The reply rate with title case bumped up to 32.3%, while lower case fell to 25.7%."[1]

Here are other *don't*s for subject lines:

- **Using a generic subject line:** Examples include something along the lines of "Hello," "Looking for Advice," and "Quick Question." Not only are these incredibly boring, but they will probably result in your email being skipped over, especially if the person is already getting a ton of emails each day.

- **Using the word "urgent":** It's unrealistic that something is urgent if you don't have an ongoing (or any) relationship yet, and saying "urgent" in the subject line makes it seem like you have no respect for the Target's time.

- **Using the word "sorry":** Doing this is problematic for two reasons. First, you should save the apologies, in life and in email, for when you actually mean it. Second, having this in the subject line means that you have to be reminded of whatever you're apologizing for every time you and the Target respond to the email.

Step Three: Use a Simple Greeting and the Person's Name

Start with something normal, not too weird, and professional: "Hi," "Hello," or something similar, and always use the person's name when you send an email. If it's a Re-RO, use the name you called the person before in real life. For a Follow-Up RO, use the same name the person used when introducing himself or herself in person. For a Borrowed Connection RO or Cool RO, use the most formal version of the person's name (for example, "Professor Tita" or "Dr. Lopez").

Step Four: Introduce Yourself and Give the World's Shortest Bio

A simple intro and short bio give the email context. Include just your first name (as your last name will be in your email signature) and a one-sentence bio. If you have multiple jobs or interests, mention only the one that is most relevant to the Reach Out. Your bio doesn't need to be your current job or role—it can also be what you want to move into.

"I'm Max, and I work at YouTube doing business development" is a great way to start if Max is looking to Reach Out to someone related to his YouTube job. But if Max wants to move into coding, he could reframe it as "I'm Max, and I'm a business development manager transitioning into coding." You are the author of your bio as well as your own PR person, so it's OK to be flexible in how you present yourself depending on the Target you are Reaching Out to.

Step Five: Offer Your Gift

Now that we are in the body of the email, it's time for the Gift. As we touched on in Chapter 4, there are at least two things you can offer the people you Reach Out to. The first is a compliment, and the second is one of the other items on the list.

- **Gift #1:** A compliment

  - Plus one additional Gift from the list below:

- **Gift #2:** An article or book recommendation your Target might like

- **Gift #3:** Knowledge you have access to that they don't or something special only you can create

- **Gift #4:** A press opportunity

- **Gift #5:** Free advice on a skill you have that would benefit them

Step Six: If Applicable, Add Your Favor

Not every email needs to include a Favor; sometimes you are just opening up a line of communication with the Target. If you do have a Favor, remember to ask a particular, definable question that can be answered easily via email. You can see Chapter 4 for more examples of good (and bad) Favors to ask a Target.

Step Seven: Write Your Closing and Add Your Email Signature

A simple and grateful "Thank you for reading this," "I appreciate your work," or "Have a nice day, [insert name here]" works well for a closing.

Below the closing, include your email signature. Create one of these for your work and personal email, and don't be afraid to tailor it to the Target. Email signatures are underappreciated as a valuable tool to position yourself in a non-pushy way to someone you don't know (in my experience, people click the links in email signatures more often than you'd think—I have a callout to Messy Bun in the signature of almost every email I send).

Regardless of whether it is sent from your personal or work email, in your email signature include some combination of:

- Your full name

- Your job title (if you like or are proud of this job) or a job-title-to-be, such as "freelance producer" (if you're still working on landing your ideal full-time job)

- Your company name, if that would be something you want to highlight in an RO

- A link to a recent project you're working on that would be impressive to the Target

- Your LinkedIn page if you want to highlight your professional experience

- Another social media account if you're especially proud of the content you share there

Email signatures should also reflect not just how *you* want people to contact you, but how *they* want to contact you as well. If you're in a service business where most of your clients call you on the phone, your signature should include your phone number.

Step Eight: Double-Check Everything, Add their Email Address, and Press "Send"!

Once your email is drafted, proofread it (a great way to do this is going sentence by sentence backward), double-check to make sure all names are spelled correctly, and finally click on any links in the email to make sure they work.

A quick note here for my type A-ers: if you notice a spelling mistake after you send it, the world will not end. When I was interviewing people for this book and asking them to pull their old emails, one (high-profile) person mused, "It was an interesting process to try and find all of the messages and some felt very embarrassing to read—one had a spelling mistake and the person still responded."

Another trap to look out for? Elana Lyn Gross, a New York City–based content strategist and writer, shares this advice: "When you are rereading your emails for typos and grammatical errors, check for words and phrases like 'just,' 'sorry,' 'I think,' and 'I feel.' These words and phrases undermine your confidence. The Gmail Plugin Just Not Sorry is a game-changer for coming across as confident and composed."

Finally, once all of the above is done, add the recipient's email to the "To:" line. This is the last thing you do when writing an email, not the first. This helps prevent accidentally sending the email before you finish typing or spell-checking it. Or worse, sending a random contact the email "Hell" because you accidently hit "Send" before you finished typing the rest of your email. Your response rate goes way down when you just mention the underworld.

Now send it off! You're done! Give yourself a pat on the back because this is a success.

> *You can't be that kid standing at the*
> *top of the waterslide, overthinking it.*
> *You have to go down the chute.*
> —TINA FEY, *BOSSYPANTS*

General Notes About the Body of Your Email

- Don't disclose anything too personal, and don't ask anything too personal.

- Don't mention anything financial or money related. As much as we'd all like to ask Bill Gates his ATM pin code, he's much more likely to offer his advice.

- In an initial Reach Out, I hate when people give times they are available to talk before I've even responded to them (there are a few exceptions here, but for the most part this is a hard-and-fast rule). Let the other person agree to meet before throwing out times that work, especially if the times you offer are superspecific ("Can we talk next Tuesday at 3:22 p.m.? That's the only time I have available all week"). You're doing the Reaching Out, not the other way around. *If* the person agrees to take it offline to a phone call, video hangout, or in-person meeting, you need to fit into *his or her* schedule.

- A Reach Out is never the place for criticism if you're working to build a relationship. It's a place to be nice. Even the most successful people are self-conscious and don't like to hear negative things about their work. There's a reason the critic in *Ratatouille* eats alone.

- Reread the email before sending and ask yourself, "What follow-up questions might someone have to this email that they would need to answer my Favor?" Anticipating one or two potential follow-ups and incorporating them into the original email will cut down on the back-and-forth.

- Keep the background info in your email to high-level details. One way to keep an email short is to ask yourself if you could read the whole thing over a voicemail. If not, edit it down.

- Keep the email conversational. In the *New York Times,* Jennifer Lawrence recounted how she Reached Out to Amy Schumer with a short and sweet email: "I emailed her after I saw 'Trainwreck' and said, 'I don't know where to get started. I guess I should just say it: I'm in love with you,'" she recalled. "We started emailing, and then emailing turned to texting."[2] When in doubt, go with your own voice. J-Law's voice is playful, and a short email that is funny is a genuine, true-to-one's place to get started.

- If you're a student, find an organic way to work that information into your bio (remember, people love to help out students). At the very least, add it to your email signature.

A NOTE ON EMAIL PRIVACY

One of the nice things about email is that it feels OK to Reach Out to someone you don't know well or at all because you have an air of privacy, and compared with replying to or mentioning someone on social media, email Reach Outs can feel more private. Of course, emails last forever, but for the most part, people don't forward nice, polite emails to other people.

But . . . I do have this note of caution: Nothing is ever truly private, so be smart here. Don't use profanity. Be respectful. Don't bash or gossip about *anyone*. You never know who is reading what you write. Judith Martin, aka the famous Miss Manners, says, "For email, the old postcard rule applies. Nobody else is supposed to read your postcards, but you'd be a fool if you wrote anything private on one."[3]

//////////////////////

TL; DR: THE EMAIL TEMPLATE OF YOUR DREAMS:

- Follow this email template when writing a Reach Out email:

  - **Step One:** Decide whether to send from your personal or work email.

  - **Step Two:** Make your subject line awesome.

  - **Step Three:** Use a simple greeting and the person's name.

  - **Step Four:** Introduce yourself and give the world's shortest bio.

  - **Step Five:** Offer your Gift.

    - » **Gift #1:** A compliment (this a must), plus:

    - » **Gift #2:** An article or book recommendation your Target might like

    - » **Gift #3:** Knowledge you have access to that they don't or something special only you can create

» **Gift #4:** A press opportunity

» **Gift #5:** Free advice on a skill you have that would benefit them

◉ **Step Six:** If applicable, add your Favor (remember that not every email needs a Favor).

◉ **Step Seven:** Write your closing and add your email signature.

◉ **Step Eight:** Double-check everything, add their email address, and press "Send"!

• Remember: Keep the email short and specific, and no email is ever truly private.

YOUR REACH OUT STRATEGY PLAN

Following the email template above, draft Reach Out emails to the Targets you identified as being your first week's Reach Outs, saving any you'd like to Reach Out to via social media until you've read the next chapter.

REACHING OUT ON SOCIAL MEDIA

E mail is a great place to anchor your Reach Out Strategy, but there are times when connecting with someone on social media makes more sense. Below are four questions you can ask yourself when you are deciding if social media is the right place to Reach Out:

- Are you already connected to the Target on social media?

- Does the Target have over 50 connections on the platform, indicating frequent use?

- Do you want to highlight something about your social media presence to the Target?

- Is the Target's email address hard to find?

If the answer is yes to two or more of these questions, Reach Out on social media instead of sending an email.

Reaching Out on social media means messaging someone on LinkedIn, Twitter, Facebook, Pinterest, Instagram, Tumblr, Snapchat, or other niche sites such as AngelList for the start-up community. Although you could engage with a Target on social media publicly on these sites by liking, commenting, or sharing their content, all popular social media sites have a private message function, which is where Reaching Out should take place. On most platforms, you need to be connected to the Target to private-message them. (Some exceptions here include Snapchat, where you can snap anyone back; Instagram, which allows you to message anyone with Instagram Direct; and LinkedIn, where you can include a customized message when you ask the Target to join your network.)

When building Messy Bun, I use Twitter to Reach Out for press coverage as most journalists are active on Twitter. I also use LinkedIn to Reach Out to potential business partners to highlight to the Target my professional history, which is probably of interest to them.

Finally, although it's not "required" for Cool ROs, I do encourage liking, commenting, or sharing the Target's content on the platform before you message them privately for a Reach Out. Sharing people's content is a good way to get on their radar before Reaching Out to them directly.

> *You can't stay in your corner of the Forest*
> *waiting for others to come to you.*
> *You have to go to them sometimes.*
> —FROM *POOH'S LITTLE INSTRUCTION BOOK*

THE TEMPLATE FOR A SOCIAL MEDIA MESSAGE

In a social media Reach Out, you'll follow loosely the same structure as the email template discussed in the previous chapter. The major difference is that social media platforms usually limit the number of characters you can send, and it's generally accepted that writing can be less formal when communicating on social media. So the template to follow here is a bit shorter, and the language you use can be more informal. You should still stay away from slang or profanity, and remember that "you" is only two letters longer than "u" and sounds 100 times more professional.

Step One: Start with a Simple Greeting and Bio

Just like with email, your social media Reach Out should contain a simple greeting, which includes a short bio to give the Target context. The bio needs to fit in a sentence, and if you have multiple jobs, interests, or passions, choose to focus on the one(s) that is the most relevant to your Reach Out.

Most social media platforms don't include subject lines in private messaging between users, but if you're Reaching Out on one that does, you can follow the tips in Chapter 7, Step Two, on subject lines.

Step Two: Offer Your Gift

As we touched on in Chapter 4, your Reach Out should include Gifts, which should answer the question "What can I give the recipient?"

- **Gift #1:** A compliment (this is a must), plus one additional Gift from the list below:
- **Gift #2:** An article or book recommendation
- **Gift #3:** Knowledge you have access to that they don't or something special only you can create
- **Gift #4:** A press opportunity
- **Gift #5:** Free advice on a skill you have that would benefit them

Step Three: If Applicable, Add Your Favor

The Favor is what, if anything, you are asking of the Target. The Favor should be tailored to the person's expertise or background and should be easy for the Target to answer quickly. (It's important to remember that certain platforms include character limits, which means that this section will usually be shorter than in an email Reach Out.)

Step Four: Include Your Email Address

Include your email address and offer to move the conversation to email if it's easier for the Target; some people check their email inbox more often than their social media messages.

Step Five: Add a Closing, Double-Check Everything, and Send!

Finally, choose a closing ("Thanks!" is fine), double-check your message for spelling errors, and confirm that all the links are correct. Then press "Send"!

A Prominent Venture Capitalist

I Am: Maria Yuan, founder of IssueVoter

The Target: Albert Wenger, managing partner at Union Square Ventures

The RO Type: Cool RO

The Backstory: I tweeted at Albert to invite him to an IssueVoter event which included a demo and conversation about "Innovation + Impact 100 Days Before the Election." I had read some of his blog entries and knew that he was personally passionate about strengthening democracy, and wrote about issues such as open government and fixing the primary system. He also had recently spoken at a "Getting Money out of Politics" event, and my tweet mentioned that.

The Reach Out (Tweet):

The Response Time: The same afternoon

The Outcome: Albert responded back to my initial tweet with his email address so I could share more about the event. Although he couldn't attend, once we switched to email he asked me smart, probing questions about IssueVoter and gave me advice on crowdfunding campaigns. I stayed in touch with Albert by keeping him updated on IssueVoter's recent progress. It's awesome how Reaching Out over Twitter, with just 140 characters, can lead to a connection!

PRIVACY NOTE FOR SOCIAL MEDIA

Of all the social media platforms, Facebook is *usually* the one that people are most hesitant about when it comes to connecting with others they don't know. For me, I'm not a huge fan of the Facebook request from someone I don't know—in fact, I specifically have my privacy settings so that only people with whom we have friends in common with can request to be my friend.

So when it comes to Facebook, you can feel free to friend people, but don't be offended if they don't accept. Nothing personal—just find their email address or Reach Out on another platform. This is also true for those who have privacy settings on their accounts; for example, if their Instagram is private, instead of requesting them and hoping they accept, find another way to contact them.

BONUS NON–SOCIAL MEDIA TIP FOR DIGITAL MARKETING PROS

You can also use Google AdWords to attract the attention of a particularly tough Target to reach. If you're failing to get the attention of someone via Reach Outs, you can always go big or go home. Buy the name of the person as a keyword on Google AdWords with a link directing the person to a landing page on your website or blog with what you want him or her to see. Because at the end of the day, we all Google our own name!

///////////////////

TL; DR: REACHING OUT ON SOCIAL MEDIA

- Email is a great place to anchor your Reach Out Strategy, but there are times when Reaching Out on social media sites rather than email makes more sense.

- Follow these five steps when writing an RO to be sent via social media:

  ◉ **Step One:** Start with a greeting and bio.

⊙ **Step Two:** Offer your Gift.

　　» **Gift #1:** A compliment, plus:

　　» **Gift #2:** An article or book recommendation your Target might like

　　» **Gift #3:** Knowledge you have access to that they don't or something special only you can create

　　» **Gift #4:** A press opportunity

　　» **Gift #5:** Free advice on a skill you have that would benefit them

⊙ **Step Three:** If applicable, add your Favor.

⊙ **Step Four:** Include your email address.

⊙ **Step Five:** Add a closing, double-check everything, and send!

YOUR REACH OUT STRATEGY PLAN

Following this social media template, draft social media Reach Outs to any of the five Targets you identified as being your first week's Reach Outs that you didn't already create a Reach Out email for in the previous chapter's prompt. You should now have the text of your Reach Out emails and social media messages completed for your first week of Reach Outs.

MANAGING A BUSY OR A QUIET INBOX

ow that you have pushed past nerves and started Reaching Out, it's time for the next somewhat scary task—checking your inbox for replies from your Targets. Remember, even if you didn't get the exact email response you were hoping for, you can try again with someone else—there are always more Reach Outs you can do.

THE FOUR MAIN TYPES OF RESPONSES

Just as there are four main types of Reach Outs, there are four main categories of Reach Out responses. Generally, your Targets will respond with one of the following:

- **Response One:** Thanks for these Gifts (this is if no Favor was asked).

- **Response Two:** Thanks for the Gifts; happy to help with your Favor.

- **Response Three:** Thanks for the Gifts; I can't help with your Favor.

- **Response Four:** Radio silence, aka no response.

Response One: Thanks for These Gifts (This Is If No Favor Was Asked)

This response is pretty straightforward. Since not all Reach Out emails need to include a Favor, this one is just the Target thanking you for the Gifts. The Targets might also add some additional info flushing out his or her thank you, depending on what Gifts you offered.

So should you reply to Response One?

To answer this question, be guided by how long the Target's response was. If the person was truly just saying thank you, there is not necessarily a reason to respond. If the length of the email was under a sentence or two, unless a direct question was asked, I usually just let it go. But if the recipient provided additional info in the form of details, wrote multiple paragraphs, or asked a question, I would respond, as it appears the Target is open to starting a bigger conversation.

With all Response Ones, since no Favor was asked, the conversation may end quickly. But if you do want to give another Gift or ask a Favor at some point down the line, at that time respond to the original email or social media message thread to show a familiarity with and long-term admiration of the Target in the future.

Response Two: Thanks for the Gifts; Happy to Help with Your Favor

Response Two is a great response—your Targets are happy to help with your Favor! They responded by answering your question in the email, asked a follow-up question, or are open to "taking it offline" to talk further. In this case, "offline" can mean anything, including a phone call, a video session, or an in-person meeting. We will get to how to handle an offline meeting soon, but first there are three Response Rules you'll follow when Targets help with your Favor: (1) respond quickly, (2) respond kindly, and (3) thank them for their help.

- **Respond quickly:** When someone replies to your Reaching Out, try your best to respond within 24 hours. Your quick response shows professionalism and dependability.

- **Respond kindly:** Reread the email before you send it and make sure it sounds nice. You want to be a joy in someone else's inbox.

- **Say thank you:** Thank the Target at both the beginning and the end of the email! Saying thank you is key to . . . everything.

Adam M. Grant, who taught us about weak and strong ties in Chapter 1, elaborated on the importance of saying thank you in his LinkedIn piece titled "6 Ways to Get Me to Email You Back":

Gratitude is more powerful than we realize. In one experiment,[1] Francesca Gino and I asked people to spend some time helping a student improve a job application cover letter. After they sent their feedback, the student replied with a message, "I just wanted to let you know that I received your feedback on my cover letter," and asked for help with another one in the next three days. Only 32% of the people helped. When the student added just eight words—"Thank you so much! I am really grateful"—the rate of helping doubled to 66%. In another experiment,[2] after people helped one student, a different student asked them for help. Being thanked by the first student boosted helping rates from 25% to 55%. The punch line: a little thanks goes a long way, not only for encouraging busy people to help you, but also for motivating them to help others like you."[3]

Besides thanking a Target via email, you could use social media to say something along the lines of "Loved hearing from @personshandle this morning—so grateful for their time and expertise!" Almost everyone secretly loves being publicly flattered. Just make sure you don't share what they said in the Reach Out, as that can be private to you both.

And what if the Target wants to move the conversation off email or social media to help you with your Favor? This is great—often, taking the conversation offline is a way for even more magic to happen.

For a phone call or video conference session, follow these tips:

- Write down three questions or topics you'd like to cover and bring them up if there is a lull in the conversation.

- Smile when you first pick up. Everyone can hear a smile in your voice (and see your smile if you're on video).

- Respect the time allotment. If the invite is for a 30-minute call, at 25 minutes start wrapping up. Always better to leave the person wanting more than to drag the conversation out until it gets awkward or you go over time.

If the person is open to setting up an in-person meeting, that's also an exciting response. But remember to be smart here: unless it's a Re-RO, keep both your personal and work physical addresses private to be safe to start. If someone asks you where you are located in order to determine a meeting place, using an approximate area is more than fine, and always meet in a public place while letting a friend know where you are going.

Beyond safety, below are some tips for meeting someone for the first time offline that will quell the awkwardness:

- If the Target doesn't suggest a specific place to get together (say, having coffee at Starbucks or meeting at the Target's office), ask your new connection to meet you at a professional event. You'll have someone to walk in with so you won't feel alone, and having an event to focus on takes the pressure off having to talk to just each other the entire time.

- Before you meet, browse the person's public social media so you can pull out any details that make sense in small talk ("Didn't you just get back from vacation last week?" or similar stuff).

- Bring a notebook and a pen. Just the act of having your notebook open and pen out while you're talking shows you believe important information will be shared, which both flatters the Target and elevates the conversation without needing to say a word.

- When it feels like the conversation is about 85 percent done and is starting to come to a natural end, start packing up or ask for the check. It is always better to leave a first meeting with the other person wanting more time with you. And nothing is worse than the conversation ending but you still have to wait for the check—so much awkwardness. Also remember that the first time you meet, the check is on you since the person is doing *you* a Favor by meeting.

- Within 24 hours, send the person a thank you email for agreeing to meet with you and include any action items or follow-ups you promised.

After meeting, look for three signs that your Targets want to stay in touch:

- They suggest another time to get together (if this happens, you're in).

- They quickly provide any follow-ups that came out of the meeting (such as sending you an article they referenced or a link to a resource site).

- They suggest someone else you should know and offer to introduce you (you are getting into their inner circle).

If any of these things happen, they seem to want to build a true connection. If they take longer and don't suggest any follow-ups, they might be too busy right now to Reach Out again right away. If that's the case, send them periodic updates to keep the connection open, but no need to overwhelm them.

Response Three: Thanks for the Gifts; I Can't Help with Your Favor

Sometimes Targets won't respond at all if they can't help with your Favor, but if a Target responds that they don't have time for your question or can't help, be gracious and email back to thank them for responding, wish them best of luck, and move on. Sometimes people just have too much on their plate; it's nothing personal. That's why we do one Reach Out every workday—more chances at bat. Not every RO will be a home run.

Response Four: Radio Silence, AKA No Response

While there is always a chance someone could surprise you and respond to a message months later, in general, if two weeks has gone by, it's unlikely you'll get a response. A quiet inbox can feel stressful, whether this is your first Reach Out or you've been Reaching Out for years. (Remember, when you send an RO every workday, you won't have the time to focus on all the different emails you've sent, so the email response anxiety decreases.)

As covered in Chapter 5, different types of Reach Outs have different response rates:

- **The Re-RO:** ~80 percent chance of response

- **The Follow-Up RO:** ~60 percent chance of response

- **The Borrowed Connection RO:** Varies greatly, depending on how strong your mutual connection is

- **The Cool RO:** ~25 percent chance of response, with variation depending on who the Target is and how effectively your message is written

You don't need to keep a tally on exact percentages like this, but you should be able to look out over the course of the Reach Outs and see clear, positive patterns emerging. If your numbers are way below the percentages outlined above (which are based on my own years of Reaching Out), taking a step back and relooking over your tactics may help. Some questions to think about to get those response rates up are:

- **The Targets:** Are you being realistic about the people you're Reaching Out to?

  - A lack of responses, especially to Borrowed Connection ROs or Cool ROs, might mean your Targets are "too big." Even if your grandpa's coworker's brother knows the president of a company you'd love to work for and she gave you permission to email her, she might just be too busy to respond. Someone in a more lateral position at the company might be a better place to start.

⊙ If you're getting a lack of response to your Cool ROs, taking a step back and focusing on Re-ROs and Follow-Up ROs for a bit will help with both your confidence and response rates, as those types of ROs tend to have a higher response rate.

- **The subject line:** Is it too boring? Did you call out something eye-catching or include your mutual connection's name? Did you use title case, meaning that every important word in the subject line is capitalized?

- **The length of the email:** Is it too long? Could you include bullets to make it clearer?

- **The Gift:** Is it genuine and personal enough? Is your Gift something the Target would actually like to receive?

- **The Favor:** Was it too large?

  ⊙ Is it short, specific, and something you can't find on Google? For example, emailing someone, "How do I start a company?" is a waste of time for everyone. It's better to use wording like "Do you have one tip for how to find customers in [specific niche]?" Putting a number on it—like "one tip"—helps the question feel more contained.

⊙ It also makes sense to double-check if what you are asking for isn't actually something the Target's clients pay for; you don't want to infringe on a revenue stream for the Target.

- **The tone of the email:** Are you being nice, complimentary, and joyful about connecting? Do you thank the Target for his or her time?

THINK BACK — WHY DIDN'T *YOU* RESPOND?

Most people have had someone Reach Out to them. Maybe it was your mom's coworker's son emailing you about moving to your city. Or maybe your second cousin's girlfriend Reached Out to you because you worked at a company she wanted to work at too and asked you to pass along her résumé as an employee referral.

Think about why you responded. It could be because you felt an obligation to know the person better, because it was a well-crafted email that intrigued you, or maybe just simply because you were in a period of your life in which you were excited to meet and help new people?

On the flip side, think about why you *didn't* respond to someone who Reached Out. Were you having a crazy month at work? Did the email get completely lost in your inbox and you couldn't find it again? Was it the day your partner broke up with you and you decided that all nonurgent email could wait while you ate ice cream?

Try not to take a lack of response personally. Sometimes you can write a great email and do all the "right things"—but maybe the Target just isn't in a time in life when he or she can take on connecting with more people. It's almost always not personal.

> *Taking initiative pays off. It is hard to visualize someone as a leader if she is always waiting to be told what to do.*
> —SHERYL SANDBERG, *Lean In*

The Nudge Update Email

You can re-email someone who didn't respond at all *if* a full four weeks has gone by. Respond to the original email thread and say something new; this is a great time to send an article or book recommendation (even if that is one of the Gifts you sent in your RO). Susie Moore, a business coach and author in New York City, says, "The magic rule successful people know? Always follow up! People are busy. Don't give up too soon. The follower-uppers in this world, win."

Think of it as a *nudge* and an *update*: the Nudge Update email. You're nudging the person to respond while providing an update or something additional that wasn't in your first email.

If the Target still doesn't respond to the Nudge Update email, move on. Reaching Out is a numbers game, and something else will pop. Keep your expectations low *and* your attitude optimistic. This works for expecting a response for Reach Outs, and for just about everything else too.

KEEPING IN TOUCH

Unlike the Nudge Update email, which you use when the Target hasn't responded at all and you can only send once, you also want to send emails to keep in touch with Targets that *do* respond.

Try to keep in touch with each person you've Reached Out to and gotten a Response One ("Thanks for the gifts") that turned into a conversation or a Response Two ("Thanks for the gifts; happy to help with your favor") about every six months.

Just remember, a "keeping-in-touch" email doesn't count as your RO for the day; you want to be doing a *new* RO each weekday. If you start counting Nudge Update or keeping-in-touch emails as your daily RO, you won't hit the goal of Reaching Out to about 260 people in a year.

The best way to remember to keep in touch with Targets is to put a note on your calendar for six months after your last email in the chain. Include the person's name and a short note about what you want to follow up with. To make your life even easier, you can attach your email chain to the reminder so you can quickly reference what you talked about and respond to that same email chain as well.

Heather Farr is a Chicago-based communications and PR manager at Reverb.com, an online marketplace for musicians. Her story indicates the power of keeping in touch with Targets over time:

> When I was a freshman in college at Ohio University studying PR, I tagged along on a networking trip to Chicago. After two full days of PR agency tours, we had a big

networking dinner with 40ish students and 20 or so professionals. It was a great event, but it seemed like there were so many people that it was hard to really connect. During dinner I sat next to Joseph Tateoka, who at the time was a Senior Account Executive at Ruder Finn. I followed up after the event to see if I could get some professional advice on how to gain some experience over the summer while working full-time in my hometown.

Heather's Reaching Out didn't end after her initial Follow-Up RO. She consistently found reasons to keep in touch even though the two didn't live in the same city.

After that initial conversation, I kept reaching out to Joseph on a regular basis: Congratulating him on a new job or promotion, seeking him out for advice about internships, or asking if he could review my résumé. To me, it was a mentorship and not something I thought could lead directly to a job. But, that changed when I decided to move to Chicago.

Once I moved, Joseph and I grabbed coffee and lunch every few months. Eventually, he ended up joining one of the biggest PR firms in the world (Edelman). Out of what appeared to be purely luck, I ended up in tech-focused PR, which was what he practiced. When the time was right, he snatched me up to work with him at Edelman. I recently left my job there, but as a direct result of a Follow-Up RO and because we stayed connected over time, Joseph went from barely an acquaintance to professional contact, to mentor, to boss, and is now a close friend.

Because Heather kept finding reasons to follow up with Joseph after meeting years earlier, he was able to hire her for the perfect job at the right time.

Ways to Restart the Conversation

When keeping in touch with Targets, always respond to the original chain so the Target has some sense, quickly, of who you are. And if it has been a while since you talked, quickly reread the chain yourself so you can be reminded of anything specific you want to call out. The actual body of the text can be slightly friendlier than the original Reach Out, and you should call the person by the name he or she used to sign the email (for example, "Elizabeth" becomes "Liz").

Just like a Nudge Update email, a keeping-in-touch email can be as short as, "Hi Keith! I saw this article on Fast Company on [topic] and thought of you because [why]: [link to article]. Hope you are enjoying the spring weather, Molly." You could also ask Keith if he's working on any projects you could help with or update Keith on the situation you asked for help with. It's a great feeling when people tell you they got their first job with the cover letter you helped them polish.

Melody Wilding, a New York City–based coach and human behavior professor, echoes this advice and shares this take on the importance of keeping in touch with Targets:

> I've built amazing relationships with readers who have Reached Out to me, implemented my advice, and then followed up weeks or even months later to let me know

about their progress. That means the world to me. Recognize that the people you're Reaching Out to want to feel validated and that sometimes the strongest way you can build a relationship with them is through consistent keeping in touch. So many people just disappear that you can easily differentiate yourself by simply following up to check in or say hello from time to time.

There's a psychological principle called the mere exposure effect which suggests that simply being repeatedly exposed to a person, thing, or idea increases our liking for it. Therefore, you can build your professional network by simply staying top of mind through relevant "touches" over time—whether that's an email to someone with a book rec, passing along an invite to a networking event, and social media is a no-brainer. Show your continued engagement and dedication to building a long-term relationship by liking, sharing, or commenting on their posts every now and then. Every time you do so, your contact is not only reminded of you (and what makes you great), but they also receive a rush of dopamine, the brain's reward chemical, which boosts their self-worth, making them associate you with feeling good.

////////////////////////

TL; DR: MANAGING A BUSY OR A QUIET INBOX

- There are four main types of responses you can get to a Reach Out:

⊙ **Response One:** Thanks for these Gifts (this is if no Favor was asked).

⊙ **Response Two:** Thanks for the Gifts; happy to help with your Favor.

⊙ **Response Three:** Thanks for the Gifts; I can't help with your Favor.

⊙ **Response Four:** Radio silence, aka no response.

- You can re-email someone who didn't respond with a Nudge Update email *if* a full four weeks has gone by.

- When Targets do respond, you'll always answer quickly, kindly, and thank them for their help. Stay in touch with Targets who responded to you by putting a note on your calendar to keep in touch with them about every six months to keep the lines of communication open.

YOUR REACH OUT STRATEGY PLAN

In your General Notes document, write down key points and to-dos from this chapter that you want to remember.

CHAPTER 10

BUT I'M ALREADY SO BUSY

If I were to go back in time and change one thing about my career, it would be to make Reaching Out a more consistent part of my life earlier. Toward the end of college and during my first few years working, I would send Reach Outs haphazardly, maybe once or twice a month at most. But I would have grown my network and probably been able to land better jobs faster if I had been as diligent about daily Reach Outs in those years as I am about them now.

The best time to plant a tree was 20 years ago.
The second best time is now.

—Famous proverb

So let's talk about how you can avoid making the latecomer mistake I made and figure out where you can make time for Reaching Out in your daily schedule, starting as soon as you finish this book.

DAILY REACH OUTS HELP
CURE RO ANXIETY

One of the reasons I advocate for one Reach Out every week-day is that it helps prevent you from getting too hung up on one Target's response. If someone doesn't write back, that's OK, because you still sent four other Reach Outs that week. It also helps Reaching Out become more of a habit if it's done daily rather than just on occasion.

Gretchen Rubin, the author of several books, including *Better Than Before* and *The Happiness Project*, wrote this about scheduling in her blog:

> One of my Secrets of Adulthood—perhaps counter-in-tuitively—is "It's often easier to do something *every day* than to do it *some days*." I post to my blog six days a week. I take notes every day. I write in my one-sentence journal every day. Many people have told me that they find it eas-ier to exercise when they exercise every day. If I try to do something four days a week, I spend a lot of time arguing with myself about whether today is the day, or tomorrow, or the next day; did the week start on Sunday or Monday; etc. And that's exhausting.[1]

Deciding you will do a Reach Out every workday will help you quit "arguing" with yourself about whether today is the day, or tomorrow is—it will just become an automatic habit.

CHOOSE A SCHEDULE THAT
WORKS FOR YOU

There are two different approaches to optimizing your schedule while sending Reach Outs. Each takes about the same amount of time, but it's when you have a pocket of time in your week that determines whether Schedule A or Schedule B works for your life.

Schedule A: Front-Load Your Reach Outs

Schedule A works best if you have one day of the week in which you have a chunk of time (about 45 minutes) to devote to Reach Outs.

- **What to do**: Choose the time during the week when you typically have some downtime. My suggestions would be Friday afternoons or Sunday nights, as these are the times when most people have space to think about the upcoming week.

    Once you've selected a time to devote to Reach Outs, use it to decide on the five Targets for the upcoming week. Find their contact info and write each of their Reach Out emails or social media messages. Either you can save them all in your draft folder and remember to send one out each morning (this works well for social media Reach Outs), or you can schedule the email Reach Outs using a free service such as Boomerang for Gmail. (Boomerang also has cool features such as Respondable, which can tell you how likely your email is to get a response by looking at the subject length, word count, question count, and more of each email you send.)

Even if you follow Schedule A, I don't recommend sending all your Reach Outs for the week at once, because if and when Targets respond, you don't want to be overloaded with responses and lose the ability to respond quickly.

- **Total time you'll need**: 45 minutes, once a week.

Schedule B: One Each Day

Schedule B works best if you have a few extra minutes you can devote each day to Reach Outs, such as in the early morning or on your lunch break. This schedule also works well if you plan on sending a lot of your Reach Outs via social media, as it can be hard to schedule social media messages in advance.

- **What to do:** Identify your Targets, find their contact info, write the message, and send one Reach Out each workday, ideally at the same time so you get into a routine. I follow Schedule B, and I typically like to do mine in the morning while I'm drinking my cup of coffee, after I've cleared my inbox of emails that have come in overnight.

- **Total time you'll need:** 8 to 10 minutes a day, 5 times a week.

BEST PRACTICES, REGARDLESS OF YOUR SCHEDULE

I try to cap my time at eight minutes per RO, but sometimes I do run over. Once you're in the groove, actually sending the Reach Outs is easy. You can create new emails or social media messages from your own previous templates by simply personalizing and customizing each RO to the Target. What takes an unexpected amount of time (and usually more mental energy) is deciding on your Targets.

Identifying Targets

To save time in identifying Targets, keep a running, portable list so you can write down whenever a Target who would help you meet your current career goals (you can always refer back to your Love/Don't Love Career list for a a refresher) crosses your mind. For me, whenever I hear someone's name or think of a new specific Target (or type of Target) I want to Reach Out to, I write it down *immediately*. My problem usually isn't a lack of people to Reach Out to; instead it's forgetting the people I was momentarily excited about contacting and then their names got lost in my brain. Get in the habit of writing down Target ideas as soon as you think of them—I keep a running list of people to RO to in both my phone's Notes app (which I use when I'm on the go) and in a draft email on my desktop (for when I'm at my desk).

Follow your curiosity and, to some extent, your jealousy (because jealousy, when used correctly, can help you see what you want more of in your *own* life). Anyone who catches your eye is a potential Target.

AN (IN)COMPLETE LIST OF PEOPLE YOU CAN RO TO INCLUDES . . .

- Someone who just had a company anniversary or got a promotion.

- Someone you interviewed with in the past.

- A podcast host or guest you admire.

- A blogger.

- An author. (If the author is hard to reach, sometimes I go through the acknowledgments to find the editor to write to instead.)

- Old coworkers.

- Someone whom you read about in a magazine or who was quoted in an article.

- An alumni board member from your college.

- A leader or higher-up at your own company.

- A recruiter at another firm.

- Someone in a similar role as you in a complimentary or competing company.

⊚ Keep in mind that people five years ahead of you and five years behind you will make up the bulk of your peer group as you move through the professional world. Knowing people in similar industries at other companies is great cross-pollination.

If you're still stuck, go through each of the four types of ROs one by one, remembering to include a variety of ROs in your plan (and keeping the Cool ROs, which have the lowest response rate, to under 20 percent of your total Reach Outs). You can also go back to Chapter 6 if you need a refresher on different ways to Reach Out to meet specific careers goals: this will help jog your brain with potential Targets too.

The Best Time to RO

Based on my experience, the ideal time is midmorning on a weekday in the Target's time zone. If that's not possible, try to keep it between 8 a.m. and 6 p.m. in the recipient's time zone (if you're not sure, default to East Coast time).

PEEK INTO THE INBOX OF:

A Re-RO That Leads to Reentry into the Workforce

I Am: Melodie Cohn, a social media specialist and writer located in Montreal

The Target: Keren Brown, a popular food writer, social media strategist, and author of *Food Lover's Guide to Seattle*

The RO Type: Re-RO

The Backstory: When little, I was friends with Keren's sister and our families were friendly with each other. I was looking to re-enter the workforce after maternity leave, and I had Keren as a friend on Instagram even though we hadn't really spoken in 20 years. I was hoping to connect for an informational interview.

The Reach Out (LinkedIn Message):

Hi Keren!

How are you?

I don't know if you remember me, I'm an old friend of Julie.

I know we spoke maybe about a year ago, but since then, I have taken part in a Career Exploration Program at the Women's Y, in Montreal, where I have been exploring my skills and passions, and have decided that I will be attending culinary school in International Gastronomy and Pastry Making and am presently researching schools to attend. I will also be starting a new foodie blog soon.

I know you are presently in Israel, but I have been following your work on Instagram (I am presently not on Facebook), and wanted to know if you would be free to Skype for an information interview or simply give me some pointers on what I can do to gain some more experience. I am really inspired by all the work you do. I think we are also friends on Pinterest.

Please let me know and thank you again for taking the time to read this message.

Best,

Melodie

The Response Time: 2 days

The Outcome: From the Reach Out conversation, I was able to negotiate a social media internship related to food with Keren that was perfect for me as I was returning from maternity leave. After the internship, I continued to work with Keren on a variety of social media and community manager projects, which provided a stepping stone for me to launch my own digital consulting business.

KEEPING TRACK OF YOUR REACH OUTS

Having a record of your Reach Outs helps you easily identify the people you've already Reached Out to. That way you're not overemailing one person, and you can also quickly figure out your rough response rates so you know how to optimize if your rates are low (see Chapter 9 if you need more help with that). A Basic Reach Out Tracker will help you do both of these things. And if you'd like to make your Reach Out Tracker more complex than just a record of your Reach Outs, you can do that too: the Career Inspiration Tracker will inspire you on your professional path, and the Project Help Tracker will allow you to quickly identify people in your network who will be helpful with a specific project or task.

Basic Reach Out Tracker

A Basic Reach Out Tracker is a spreadsheet that generally includes columns for:

- The date the Reach Out was sent

- The Target's name

- The Target's job title or company

- The contact method (email, Twitter, LinkedIn, other)

- The Reach Out type (Re-RO, Follow-Up RO, Borrowed Connection RO, Cool RO)

- A brief description of the email, including the Gift(s) and Favor

- The date a response was received (remember, it's OK to follow up with a Nudge Update email if a response is not received after four weeks)

- The outcome

- Any additional notes

Career Inspiration Tracker

If you're looking for a tracker that will inspire you as you plot out your next few career moves, you can jazz up the Basic

Reach Out Tracker to create the Career Inspiration Tracker. People just starting out in the workforce or looking to make big career shifts will find the Career Inspiration Tracker especially helpful.

For the Career Inspiration Tracker, first include all the columns that are on the Basic Reach Out Tracker (you can leave the Reaching Out rows blank if you haven't Reached Out yet). Then insert additional columns based on where the Targets went to school, what their first job was, what certificate programs they have done, where they are located, and/or more based on your career goals. It will also be helpful here to include their LinkedIn profile, company bio, or, if you've already emailed with them, information they have shared with you. Studying and identifying potential patterns in these extra columns among people in your industry whom you admire will inspire you to emulate those patterns and help you figure out what your next step might be.

Alana Strassfield developed and used the Career Inspiration Tracker when figuring out her next career move. She says of her experience:

> The Career Inspiration Tracker helped me see the trends in both work and educational experiences of the people who I aspired to be professionally. I clearly saw, in both job descriptions that I was applying to and in my spreadsheet, that people in my desired field typically had several years of international experience in addition to having a master's degree. I noted their experience was typically with a business or governmental agency as op-

posed to NGO work. I knew it would be difficult to get an overseas position early on in my career, but being aware of their track records encouraged me to Reach Out to people outside of my field who had worked abroad.

I used the Re-RO to connect with a friend from high school in the engineering field who had spent significant time working in several countries internationally, including China. She provided great insight into China's political landscape around human rights and let me know which cities would be most viable for job opportunities. Among others, she encouraged me to continue searching and eventually make the leap given the right opportunity.

Alana provided this quote writing from Shanghai, China, where she is now in her dream job focusing on corporate social responsibility—awesome!

Project Help Tracker

On the other hand, if you're looking for a tracker that will help organize your network so you can quickly see who can help you with specific tasks, you can also jazz up the Basic Reach Out Tracker to create the Project Help Tracker. People who are entrepreneurs, small business owners, or are in roles that require knowing lots of people across a variety of companies will find the Project Help Tracker a great fit. This is the tracker I am using while building and launching Messy Bun.

The Project Help Tracker allows you to quickly identify people in your network who will be helpful with a specific project or task, whether or not you have Reached Out to them yet.

For the Project Help Tracker, first include all the columns that are on the Basic Reach Out Tracker (you can leave the Reaching Out rows blank if you haven't Reached Out yet). Then insert additional columns based on what an individual's area of expertise is, how the person could possibly help you now or in the future, and what Borrowed Connected ROs the person might offer to accelerate your career or company's growth.

Diana Murakhovskaya and Irene Ryabaya, the cofounders of Monarq, used the Project Help Tracker when they started building their company that focuses on funding women-led start-ups. They had decided to put themselves through a crash course of going to two start-up networking events a night for six months. They were meeting dozens of terrific people, but just collecting business cards wasn't going to be a good system of remembering everyone. So to keep track of their new connections, they started a Project Help Tracker. With this method, something that used to take weeks, such as finding a new start-up–focused lawyer, now took just hours. All they had to do was look through their Project Help tracker until they found someone who specialized in start-up law or had connections to a great start-up lawyer and Reach Out, filling out the rows about the Reach Out as they did.

Creating a Tracker That Works for You

Ultimately, you want to find the parts from each tracker that work best for you and customize accordingly to meet your specific RO goals. For example, you could have multiple tabs within one Basic Reach Out Tracker for each career goal you're currently pursuing, you could combine a pared-down version of the Career Inspiration and Project Help Trackers into one spreadsheet, or you could keep a running list of potential Targets as part of your tracker on a separate tab.

To get you started, you can find examples of each tracker at reachoutstrategy.com/tracker.

//////////////////////

TL; DR: BUT I'M ALREADY SO BUSY

- The cornerstone of Reach Out Strategy is that you Reach Out to someone new every single weekday, with no end date in sight.

- This approach both makes Reaching Out a habit *and* helps so you don't get too hung up on one person's response. The more ROs you send, the less emotionally invested you will get into each response or nonresponse.

- There are two different approaches to optimizing your time while sending Reach Outs:

  - **Schedule A:** Front-load your Reach Outs. This works best if you have one day of the week in which you have some free time to think and plan.

  - **Schedule B:** Do one Reach Out each day. This works best if you have a few extra minutes you can devote each day.

- The ideal time to send a Reach Out is midmorning on a weekday in the Target's time zone.

- Keep track of your Reach Outs as you move towards your career goals via a Basic Reach Out Tracker, a Career Inspiration Tracker, or a Project Help Tracker.

YOUR REACH OUT STRATEGY PLAN

Choose one of the time management systems (Schedule A or B) to follow for your Reach Outs and begin making arrangements to implement it for the upcoming week by blocking off the time on your calendar.

Then, decide how you want to keep track of your Reach Outs, and create a tracker customized to your goals. To get you started, you can find examples of the Basic Reach Out Tracker, the Career Inspiration Tracker, and the Project Help Tracker at http://www.reachoutstrategy.com/tracker.

TAKING IT TO
THE NEXT LEVEL

CHAPTER 11

NEXT STEPS

You did it! By following the prompts at the end of each chapter, you've developed your own personalized Reach Out Strategy Plan that has both your long-term career goals *and* the practical pieces you need for your first full week of executing your specific Reach Out Strategy.

If you follow your Reach Out Strategy Plan and Reach Out to one person every business day, in one year you'll have Reached Out to about 260 people. 260! And assuming a response rate around 40 percent, you will have gotten around 104 responses. That's over *a hundred people* you've talked to over the past year that you wouldn't have if you didn't start a Reach Out Strategy!

> *You can be the lead in your own life.*
> —KERRY WASHINGTON, *GLAMOUR* MAGAZINE

FINAL NOTES

Now that we have your Reach Out Strategy Plan done, there are a few final things to cover before we finish our time together. In this chapter, we'll be looking at what to do when *you're* someone else's Target, how to introduce two people via email, and how to start a book club for Reaching Out (really!).

How to Become Someone Else's Target

Positioning yourself to be a good Target for others to Reach Out to is one of the smartest things you can do to grow your influence—now opportunities will be coming to you instead of you going to them. You want to be seen as being open to being the Target of someone else's Reach Out, so make your email address, or any other way you prefer to be contacted, easily visible on all the platforms you are active on.

After a few months of Reaching Out with others, you'll have a larger network and you will probably find yourself starting to be the Target of other people's Reach Outs more often, especially through Borrowed Connection ROs. And now that you know everything it takes to be the person sending a Reach Out, how could you be anything but kind?

What to Do When *You* Start Getting Reach Outs

When you're the Target of others' Reach Outs, you want to be two things: responsive and joyful.

First, a fast reply to someone's Reach Out is one of the easiest ways to be seen as responsive, which is a hugely valued trait in the workplace. This will earn you more invites socially too, as faster communication to invitations makes you look more interested in receiving them.

Adelle Platon, an editor at *Billboard* who covers R&B and hip-hop news, knows how important being responsive is. She attempts to respond to each email she's sent within 10 seconds! Even if you're not as on top of your inbox as Adelle, it's not 1998—emails don't get lost, and computers work fine. So if you get an email, you need to respond to it. As for social media, many platforms show when you've read someone's message, so keep that in mind as well. (Nothing's worse than seeing someone read your Twitter direct message and is just waiting a few days to respond!)

Second, being joyful about connecting is one of the best ways to guarantee more connections. When you are happy someone Reached Out to you, tell the person. A quick note that says "Can't believe how thrilled I was to get a connection request from you!," "Seeing your name in my inbox made my Monday," or even a simple "I was thrilled to get this email" is a great way to highlight that you appreciate that the person thought of you as a Reach Out Target.

How to Introduce Two People via Email

If you don't have time or you're not the right person to help someone who Reached Out to you, you can offer an introduction to someone else who might be a better fit. Or, as we know from Chapter 4, an introduction offer can also be a Gift. There are two basic options to connect people via email: Option One is the option I recommend in 99 percent of cases.

- **Option One:** Introduce the person who Reached Out to you to the other person on the same email—after you made sure this was OK with both parties. Once they are connected, give them permission to move you to BCC.

  - **Pro:** You get to write a glowing connection email that will make both people feel good: "DJ, this is Stephanie. DJ is the most amazing big sister ever, and Stephanie is the cutest middle sister ever . . ."

  - **Con:** It takes slightly more work. You have to take the time to ask both people for their permission to connect them, and you have to take the time to write an introduction email.

  - **Verdict:** The extra time is worth it to make sure you aren't frustrating the people in your network by connecting them to people they are not interested in being connected to. Use this method.

- **Option Two:** Give the person who Reached Out to you the email address of the other person. In this case, you would say something along the lines of "Tell Marco I sent you."

  - **Pro:** This is the easiest for you. You don't have to Reach Out to the potential connection for permission to share his or her email address, nor do you have to write an introduction email.

⊚ **Con:** It's not personal and can be annoying to the person whose email address you just gave out without asking permission first.

⊚ **Verdict:** Skip it—the only exception when it comes to sharing emails without the other party's permission is if the Target is providing a service and this person would be a potential new paying client for the Target.

PEEK INTO THE INBOX OF:

Someone Who Can Give You an Internship

I Am: Mimi Zheng, a world traveler, writer, and business development consultant

The Target: Smit Patel, former Growth Marketer at Scriptrock and currently doing business development/partnerships at Datadog

The RO Type: Cool RO

The Backstory: It was late April 2013 and I still wasn't sure what I would do after college graduation. I was torn between finding a full time job in the Boulder/Denver area, traveling the world for a few months, or doing an internship in Silicon Valley. For a few months, I'd been re-reading Smit Patel's blog post on landing a start-up internship through the use of different tactics and strategies. Even though Smit was an eighteen-year-old high school senior who didn't have any experience, his persistence eventually landed him an internship with a Y Combinator company in Silicon Valley. One day, I decided to reach out to him on Twitter.

The Reach Out Tweet:

> **Mimi Zheng**
> @mimizheng01
>
> @thesmitpatel Been following your blog posts. Super helpful! I've been utilizing your tips. Would love to connect. :)
>
> 3:51 PM - 30 Apr 2013

The Response Time: Right away

The Outcome: We ended up emailing that same day and then doing a Google video chat 11 days later. During our Google chat, I learned that he was now 19 and doing marketing for a 500 Startups company called Scriptrock in Silicon Valley. And as fate would have it, they were looking for a new Marketing intern! I had no idea what the "DevOps" space was at the time, but Scriptrock seemed interesting and this was an unexpected opportunity that I couldn't pass up. Smit wanted writing samples, so I sent them an hour after our conversation. Things happened quickly and 2 days later, I interviewed with the CEO of the company and Smit. The CEO asked me about my previous work done and had me work on an assignment. I was asked to research their top 5 competitors and understand the potential of the space in the next 5 years. I worked on it over the days that followed, crossed my fingers, and sent off my assignment.

Scriptrock hired me 3 days later, flew me out to San Francisco 3 days after that, and had me start my internship just 2 days later. Looking back, I'm glad I took a chance and acted fast. Because of that tweet, I was able to not only land an internship, but have the opportunity to learn, grow, and network in Silicon Valley, ultimately leading to me starting my own consulting company.

Start Your Own Reach Out Initiative

Are you feeling so inspired by your Reach Outs that you want to get your friends and coworkers in on the fun? Then start your own Reach Out Initiative (ROI). It's like a book club with no lying about whether you read the book.

You'll need:

- Anywhere from 2 to 10 participants. You can do this with just your best friend or with your whole team at work. If you have over 10 participants, I'd break into smaller groups.

- A team leader. This could be you!

- Access to a joint spreadsheet (e.g., a Google sheet).

- Interest in furthering your career goals.

Step One: How Long Does This Last?
Have everyone decide on a time frame to run the ROI; I'd recommend between four and eight weeks to start.

Step Two: Be SMART

Each participant needs to develop one SMART (specific, measurable, achievable, relevant, and time-bound) goal just for the initiative that Reaching Out can help the person achieve.

Sample goals:

- I want to have an informational interview with three people who work at companies I admire in the next month.

- I want to have coffee with five people who live in my new city in the next two months.

- I would like to ask six writers I admire for their best tip for a new journalist.

Step Three: Remember, If You Can't Measure It, You Can't Manage It

We talked about the importance of Reach Out Trackers in Chapter 10; you can also find example trackers at http://www.reachoutstrategy.com/tracker. Lynn Daue, a Maryland-based personal development author, has run multiple Reach Out Initiatives with her community. She shares why she encourages the members of her community to track their Reach Outs: "Reach Out Trackers help participants understand how their efforts are landing in the real world. What we focus on grows, so if participants focus on their Reach Out successes, then they're more likely to have successful Reach Outs in the future."

Step Four: Buddy Up

Everyone in the group should get paired up with an accountability buddy to hold each other accountable for the one Reach Out per workday. Your ROI can be done completely online, or it can be done in person with weekly check-ins with your buddy. Whether in person or online, a simple "Hey Noah, I did 3 ROs this week so far! How many did you do?" is all it takes to be a buddy.

Step Five: Reward Yourself!

At the end of the Reach Out Initiative, the people who have met their ROI goal can celebrate with a fun group activity—maybe a dinner where people bring as a guest a new person they have met through the process, or bring their best or coolest Reach Out story to share with the group, or maybe just bring some treats to celebrate their networks expanding!

/////////////////////

TL; DR: BUT I'M ALREADY SO BUSY

- If you Reach Out to one person every business day, in one year you'll have Reached Out to about 260 people. Assuming a response rate of around 40 percent, you will have gotten around 104 responses. That's *a hundred people* you've talked to over the past year that you wouldn't have if you didn't start a Reach Out Strategy.

- Make your email address, or any other way you prefer to be contacted, easily visible on all the platforms you are active on so you can be the Target of others' Reach Outs; now opportunities can start coming to you.

- When you do become the Target of others' Reach Outs, you want to be responsive and joyful.

- When you're introducing two people via email, in most cases you will introduce them on the same email after you have OK'd it with both parties, giving them permission to move you to BCC.

- You can start your own Reach Out Initiative (ROI) with your friends and coworkers to motivate each other to grow your networks.

YOUR REACH OUT STRATEGY PLAN

In your General Notes document, write down key points and to-dos from this chapter that you want to remember.

A FINAL NOTE FROM ME

You have to be out there to get noticed. You have to volunteer to stand in the spotlight. You have to raise your hand. You have to send the first email.

You still might fail to be noticed if you do these things. But you definitely won't be noticed if you wait for someone else to Reach Out to you.

So . . . what are you waiting for?

Reach Out. Reach Out. Reach Out.

Reach Out today.

HOW BUSY PEOPLE MANAGE THEIR INBOX

Now that you have finished your own personalized Reach Out Strategy Plan, it's time to start putting it into action. As you do, your inbox probably will become busier with more incoming emails and social media message notifications. As we learned in Chapter 11, responding to messages quickly makes you look responsible and professional and could give you better access to time-sensitive opportunities. As Newman said on *Seinfeld*, "The mail never stops!"—so we all might as well stay on top of it.

Below are tips and tricks from professionals across a variety of industries and locations who have learned how to tackle their inbox to prevent email overload. I hope several of these tips will be applicable to your own inbox situation.

SAVE IT FOR FRIDAY

I do two things to manage my email. (1) I have a "Deal with on Friday" folder. When something doesn't require an immediate response, I move it to that folder and—you guessed it!—I answer everything in that folder on Friday. (2) When an email is related to a task with a deadline, I do not move it out of my inbox until that task is complete. I usually only have 3–5 emails in my inbox and I'm constantly working towards inbox zero. Plus, completing those tasks so I can move that email out of my inbox serves as a great motivator!

—Sarah Von Bargen, a Minnesota-based blogger
   and writer at Yesandyes.org

THE TWO-MINUTE RULE

I have a two-minute rule when I am on the go. If I see an email I can respond to in under 2 minutes I do it on the spot to avoid "to-do" list build-up. For anything deeper I like to respond to emails in a set period—typically late morning—and then again after lunch (rather than respond to everything the second it hits my inbox). I don't want other people's agendas ruling my day. I also have 4 inboxes so I can't check them obsessively—I'd get nothing done! Also—not every email warrants a response. I also rarely respond to emails after 7 or 8PM for my own sanity— a lot of requests are far less urgent than you think.

—Susie Moore, a New York City–based business
   coach and author

ONLY THE ABSOLUTES

I have a simple rule for managing my inbox—I never check email on my phone unless I absolutely have to do so. Why? In my experience, items that require urgent attention are very quickly migrating to text messages or a tool like Slack. I'm able to reply 10x more quickly to emails with a keyboard, and I use assistant.to (an awesome free tool for Gmail) to eliminate back and forth on meeting scheduling.

> —Spencer X. Smith, a Wisconsin-based entrepreneur who helps professional services practices do better business development with social media

RESPOND TO *EVERYTHING*

I think emails are incredibly important. I respond to every single one, even if it's just a "hello." There are two keys to managing any inbox. (1) Commit to dedicating a certain amount of time to responding to emails. It changes over time with my schedule, but right now I find that spending three to five hours every morning getting through emails is the best way for me to stay on top of them. (2) Come up with a system that works for you. I read my emails as they come in on my phone, but as a rule, I don't respond until I'm sitting at my computer. Instead, I use the "star" feature to collect the ones I need to respond to or ones I need to "keep on file." My "starred emails" essentially become my to-do list for the next day.

> —Carly A. Heitlinger, a Connecticut-based blogger at thecollegeprepster.com

TAKE IT OFFLINE

The reason email is so easy to avoid is because it's so easy to ignore. Most of us get an avalanche in our inbox and hide from the communication instead of engaging with it, which is the whole point! I find the best approach to anything is the take action approach, so if it's an ongoing thread I need to stay on top of, I schedule a call to address everything at once, which tends to be much more thorough and much quicker than the back and forth.

—Bea Arthur, a New York City–based therapist and
founder of the mental health think tank The Difference

20-MINUTE BREAKS

Carve out 20 minutes in the morning, mid-day, and evening to do a quick clean of your inbox by briefly responding to those emails which require responses, sending a "let me get back to you," or forwarding the email onwards to someone who can best respond. This way, your inbox remains clean and most importantly you are never overwhelmed.

—Shinjini Das, a San Francisco–based founder and
CEO of The Das Media Group

TAKE ACTION IMMEDIATELY

There are no emails in my inbox. Once I get an email, I read it, decide whether it needs action, and either sort it or delete it. If it needs action, I star it. In this way, my starred items become my to-do list. If it's something I don't need to respond to, I move it to a folder for later reference. I keep most emails in case I need to review them later, unless they're spam. The great thing about this system is that I can make it work on my phone, too.

> —Briana Morgan, an Atlanta-based author
> of young adult fiction

USE ORGANIZING CATEGORIES

I usually get on average 50 emails a day, which isn't too bad. In order to keep everything organized I have many different categories and sub-categories within the "Inbox" of Outlook. Examples of categories include: Completed Shipments. Sales Team, Vendors, Inquiries, Events, Content, and Trade/ Professional Organizations. Within each of these categories is a sub-category. As an example, the category for "Events" will show: the date of the event, which sales rep is hosting the event, and the name of the event. Having multiple sub-categories in each folder is absolutely necessary in order to stay on top of my tasks.

> —Daniel Skaritka, a New York–based marketing
> coordinator at ENECON Corporation

BUSINESS HOURS ONLY

I only answer emails during normal business hours. I have to make sure my clients don't get the feeling of me providing my services "on demand." That's a boundary lesson with email that took a long time to learn, but it has made my work life balance much more effective.

> —Catherine Whitcher, an Illinois-based special needs
> education and community advocate

ALWAYS INBOX ZERO

I'm obsessive about maintaining a ZERO inbox. Each day, I power through 100 or more emails and end the day with an empty inbox. One technique I use to maintain zero inbox discipline is to schedule my email to automatically check once every 30 minutes, instead of the default 5–10 minutes. That allows me to batch responses between longer, uninterrupted work sessions.

> —Kent Lewis, the Oregon-based president and founder
> of Anvil Media, a measurable marketing agency, and
> pdxMindShare, a career community

YOUR REACH OUT STRATEGY PLAN—REVIEW

'd recommend that you revisit your Reach Out Strategy Plan as your career goals change. For me, this is about every six months. The best way to do this is to return to this Appendix and whip up a new Reach Out Strategy Plan in line with your updated career goals.

For easy reference, here are all the Reach Out Strategy Plan prompts from each chapter. As you work on your updated Reach Out Strategy Plan from these prompts, you can flip back to the chapter of any prompt that is giving you trouble for a quick refresher on the concepts in that chapter.

CHAPTER 1

Write your favorite motivational quote at the top of your Reach Out Strategy Plan so that you're inspired every time you review your plan.

CHAPTER 2

Choose three adjectives or phrases that you want to be known for and make sure these descriptors are reflected across your social media profiles, the content you share online, and the text of the Reach Outs you send.

CHAPTER 3

First, finish this sentence and put it in your Reach Out Plan: "My biggest fear when Reaching Out is _____. The way I will push past that fear is by _____."

Next, using your Love/Don't Love list, choose two to four career goals you'd like to focus on in the next six months and brainstorm a list of at least six Targets that could help make your goals a reality.

CHAPTER 4

Chose five of your top Targets from the brainstormed list you wrote down in the Chapter 3 prompt. Under each Target, write down at least two Gifts you could provide for each of them and, if needed, one Favor you could ask from each of them. If you can't think of unique Gift(s) to give or a Favor to ask for, choose a different Target in their place. This question of "Do I have a unique Gift and/or a Favor to ask of them?" will help cut down the long list of brainstormed Targets created in Chapter 3's prompt. Once you have five Targets with Gifts and/or Favors for each, these are your first week's Reach Outs.

CHAPTER 5

Mark each of the five Targets you've identified as your first week's Reach Outs as being a Re-RO, Follow-Up RO, Borrowed Connection RO, or Cool RO, being sure to have a mix of all four. Then find their contact information and put that next to each Target's name.

CHAPTER 6

Looking at your career goals developed in Chapter 3 from your Love/Don't Love list, take any applicable notes from this chapter and either slightly tweak your Reach Out Strategy Plan to make sure it accurately reflects these goals or write down items to remember and to-dos in a General Notes document as inspiration as you move toward your future.

CHAPTER 7

Following the email template in this chapter, draft Reach Out emails to the Targets you identified as being your first week's Reach Outs.

CHAPTER 8

Following the social media template in this chapter, draft social media Reach Outs to any of the five Targets you identified as being your first week's Reach Outs that you didn't already create a Reach Out email for.

CHAPTER 9

In your General Notes document, write down key points and to-dos from this chapter that you want to remember.

CHAPTER 10

Choose one of the time management systems (Schedule A or B) to follow for your Reach Outs and begin making arrangements to implement it for the upcoming week by blocking off the time on your calendar. Then, decide how you want to keep track of your Reach Outs and create a tracker customized to your goals. To get you started, you can find examples of the Basic Reach Out Tracker, the Career Inspiration Tracker, and the Project Help Tracker at http://www.reachoutstrategy.com/tracker.

CHAPTER 11

In your General Notes document, write down key points and to-dos from this chapter that you want to remember.

ACKNOWLEDGMENTS

There are many people who helped make this book happen for me. I can't thank them all, but I'll try my best:

To my *Smart, Pretty, & Awkward* readers, whose generous support of my writing gave me my first glimpse into the power of digital, ultimately leading to this book. I would not have achieved my goal of someday writing a book without each of you.

To Denise Restauri and Forbes for letting me write the "Mentoring Moments" column that introduced Reaching Out to the world.

To Mollie Glick and her team at CAA for their invaluable expertise in placing the book in the capable editorial hands of Cheryl Ringer, her team at McGraw-Hill, and Audible.

To everyone who provided stories or interviews for this manuscript, even the ones that didn't make the final draft. Your willingness to share your experiences helped shape this book, and I will be forever indebted; please don't hesitate to Reach Out whenever I can help you with your projects as you have done for me.

To Christina Vuleta for being my New York fairy godmother, always.

To Jocelyn Bonneau, Weezie Mackey, Vivian Nunez, and Sarah Von Bargen for being my early readers and giving wonderful feedback.

To Katie Nolan and Elizabeth Stokely for being the original crew.

To the extended Ford, Mackey, and Beck families for all their support. I have the best family around me—both the one I was born into and the one I married into.

To Dad because even if my last name changed, my heart didn't. When people say I'm "such a Ford," I puff up with pride.

To Mom because this book exists almost solely because you always believed it would, and never let me forget that. You are the real MVP.

To Teri, the best little sister in the world. Even if we weren't related, you know I would still try desperately to make you be my friend.

And finally to Collin for always being the guy who comes through. In a thousand different ways you've enriched my life forever because it's tied to yours. Marrying you was the choice I feel proudest of and most grateful for every day. And to the little baby who has been kicking in my stomach for most of these final edits: your dad and I cannot wait to meet you. We hope that you know how much we already love you and want to do right raising you. The world is wide, waiting, and yours, little one.

With gratitude, Molly

P.S. If you've read this far, reader, here's one extra piece of advice that has carried me through life. It's from my Papa, who I so wish was here to hold this book in his hand: "Never talk down to anyone. And never let anyone talk down to you."

You got this!

NOTES

Introduction

1. *Disclosure:* Permission was granted by the senders of the emails and social media messages for Molly to include their conversations. The sender of each interaction self-reported the contents of the discussion and the story around it.

Chapter 1

1. http://money.usnews.com/money/blogs/outside-voices-careers/2015/10/07/7-things-you-should-know-about-employee-referrals.
2. https://www.linkedin.com/pulse/20130617112202-69244073-finding-the-hidden-value-in-your-network.
3. Granovetter's study, http://www.jstor.org/stable/2776392.
4. More info on this concept is here: https://hbr.org/2005/12/how-to-build-your-network.

Chapter 2

1. https://business.linkedin.com/content/dam/business/marketing-solutions/global/en_US/campaigns/pdfs/Linkedin_SophGuide_020314.pdf.
2. http://greatday.com/motivate/970114.html
3. http://www.forbes.com/sites/jacquelynsmith/2013/04/26/why-every-job-seeker-should-have-a-personal-website-and-what-it-should-include.

Chapter 3

1. SMART first appeared in the November 1981 issue of *Management Review*. Sometimes you might hear slight variations of the acronym.

Chapter 5

1. https://www.linkedin.com/pulse/20130617112202-69244073-finding-the-hidden-value-in-your-network. More information on dormant tie research can be found here: http://sloanreview.mit.edu/article/the-power-of-reconnection-how-dormant-ties-can-surprise-you/.

Chapter 6

1. http://www.oprah.com/omagazine/what-i-know-for-sure-hard-work.
2. http://www.npr.org/2012/06/11/154753767/joan-rivers-hates-you-and-everyone-else.
3. http://www.newyorker.com/culture/culture-desk/seeing-nora-everywhere.

Chapter 7

1. http://www.fastcompany.com/3062538/data-backed-strategies-for-writing-subject-lines-that-get-your-email-read.
2. http://artsbeat.blogs.nytimes.com/2015/08/26/jennifer-lawrence-amy-schumer-writing-screenplay-together/.
3. https://www.wired.com/1997/11/manners/.

Chapter 9

1. http://psycnet.apa.org/journals/psp/98/6/946/ .
2. Ibid.
3. https://www.linkedin.com/pulse/20130624114114-69244073-6-ways-to-get-me-to-email-you-back.

Chapter 10

1. http://gretchenrubin.com/happiness_project/2012/04/proposed-resolution-do-something-every-day/.

INDEX

ABOUT THE AUTHOR

Molly Beck is the founder of the podcast creation site Messy Bun; creator of the lifestyle blog *Smart, Pretty & Awkward*; and a marketing expert who has provided digital strategies for numerous companies, including Forbes, Venmo, Rice University, and Hearst. Her work has been featured in *Business Insider, Parade, Refinery29, Lifehacker,* the *Boston Globe,* and more. Follow Beck on social media at @MsMollyBeck on all platforms.